Cyber Security Overview for Absolute Beginners

A beginner's guide to Cyber Security

FARHADUR RAHIM

ISBN: 9798859472710

WHAT WILL YOU LEARN?

In Chapter 1, you will learn on the internet so call cyber space.

In Chapter 2, you will learn about hackers, classification or categories of hackers, understanding cracker.

In Chapter 3, you will learn about malwares, various purposes of malwares, types of malwares in cyber-attacks and similar use cases.

In Chapter 4, you will learn all about cybercrimes, categories, different types of cybercrimes, impact in our society.

In Chapter 5, you will learn about authentication in cybersecurity. Ensuring digital identity and security understanding authentication, The importance of authentication, methods of authentication, authentication in action.

In Chapter 6, you will learn in detail about encryption in cybersecurity, how does encryption work, benefits and use cases.

In Chapter 7, you will learn about digital signatures in cybersecurity, The consequence of digital signatures, applications in real-world.

In Chapter 8, you will learn about Antivirus in Cybersecurity, The importance of antivirus, applications in real-world.

In Chapter 9, you will learn about understanding firewalls, firewall mechanisms: how they work, the importance of firewalls: safeguarding digital frontiers applications in real-world.

In Chapter 10, you will learn about steganography and little more about the significances of steganography.

In Chapter 11, you will learn about investigating cybercrimes: introduction to computer forensic, computer forensic applications and impact, challenges and future trends.

In Chapter 12, you will learn about various certifications on cyber security. Learn about certified ethical hacker (CEH), Comptia Security+, CISSP and more.

DEDICATION

This book is dedicated to beginners who are interested in learning about cyber security and ethical hacking. This book is primarily intended for Application developers, Programmers, Software Engineers, DevOps, IT managers, technology architects, Teachers and Students who study in IT. If you are also ready to learn about new technologies, then this book is ideal for you.

To all those who tirelessly strive to protect the digital realm. Your dedication, attention, and expertise in the field of cyber security are an encouragement of hope in an interconnected world. May your efforts continue to boost our defenses, secure our data, and preserve the integrity of the digital landscape for generations to come.

CONTENTS

What will you learn?   iii

Overviews   ix

1   **Chapter 1**   1
    Introduction to Cyberspace
    The History of Internet   2
    Cybersecurity Models   3
    Cyber Attacks: Threats, Techniques, and   5
    Mitigation   5
    Exploring the Various Types of Cybercrime   6
    Impact of Cyber Attacks
    The Significance of Cybersecurity

2   **Chapter 2**   10
    Hacker and Their Jobs
    What is Hacking   11
    Classified or Categories of Hackers   12
    Understanding Crackers   14

3   **Chapter 3**   15
    Overview Malware   15
    Types of Malware   16
    Purpose of Malware   16
    How Malware Works   18
    Difference between Malware and Virus   22

4   **Chapter 4**   27
    Understanding Cybercrime   27
    Categories of Cybercrime   28
    Types of Cybercrime   30
    Impact of Cybercrime on Society   30

5   **Chapter 5**   **36**
    Authentication in Cybersecurity:
    Ensuring Digital Identity and Security   36
    Understanding Authentication   37
    The Importance of Authentication   40
    Methods of Authentication   72
    Authentication in Action:
    A Glimpse into Secure Digital Interactions   76

6   **Chapter 6**   **44**
    Encryption in Cybersecurity:
    Securing the Digital World with Unbreakable   44
    Shields   46
    Understanding Encryption   47
    How Does Encryption Work?
    Exploring the Best Encryption Algorithms: 78
    Building a Fortified Digital Defense   83
    Best Practices for Encryption

7   **Chapter 7**   **50**
    Digital Signatures in Cybersecurity:
    Fortifying Identity and Trust   51
    Understanding Digital Signatures   52
    How Digital Signatures Work   89
    The Consequence of Digital Signatures   93
    Applications in Real-World   98

8   **Chapter 8**   102
    Antivirus in Cybersecurity:
    The Shield Against Malicious Intrusions   102
    How does it work?   103
    The Importance of Antivirus   104
    Applications in Real-World   106

9   **Chapter 9**   110
    The Guardian at the Gateway:

Understanding Firewalls 110

Firewall Mechanisms: How They Work 112

The Importance of Firewalls:
Safeguarding Digital Frontiers 117

Applications in Real-World 120

Challenges and Considerations 121

Chapter 10 123

Introduction to Steganography 123

The Significances of Steganography 125

Chapter 11 128

Investigating cybercrimes:
Introduction to Computer forensic 128

Computer Forensic Applications and Impact 132

Challenges and Future Trends 135

Chapter 12 137

Certifications on Cyber Security 137

Certified Ethical Hacker 139

Comptia Security+ 140

CISSP 141

Other Certifications 142

Conclusion

About Author 148

Cyber Security Overview for Absolute Beginners

ACKNOWLEDGMENTS

Writing a book is a journey that involves the support, encouragement, and contributions of numerous individuals and entities. As I stand on the threshold of completing this endeavor, I am filled with gratitude for the many people who have made this book possible.

First and foremost, I would like to express my heartfelt gratitude to my family, whose unwavering love and understanding provided me with the time and space to bring my ideas to life. Your support has been a constant source of inspiration.

I extend my sincere appreciation to my friends and colleagues who provided valuable feedback, brainstormed ideas, and offered their insights throughout the writing process. Your perspectives have enriched the content of this book immensely.

I am immensely thankful to the experts and professionals who graciously shared their expertise and experiences, allowing me to present accurate and informed insights within these pages. Your willingness to share your knowledge is deeply appreciated.

A special acknowledgment goes to my mentor, whose guidance and wisdom have been invaluable on this journey. Your encouragement pushed me to strive for excellence in every chapter.

To the editorial and publishing teams who worked tirelessly to shape this book into its final form, I extend my gratitude for your dedication to quality and precision.

Last but not least, I would like to thank the readers, whose curiosity and interest in this book give purpose to my writing.

This book is a testament to the collective effort and support of all those mentioned above and many more whose names may not appear here. Your contributions, no matter how small, have left an indelible mark on this work. Thank you for being a part of this journey.

With sincere appreciation,

Farhadur Rahim

OVERVIEWS

Cybersecurity is the practice of protecting digital systems, networks, devices, and data from malicious attacks, unauthorized access, and potential threats. In an increasingly connected world, where technology is integral to our daily lives, understanding the basics of cybersecurity is essential for everyone, from individuals to businesses. This overview provides a foundational understanding of key concepts in cybersecurity for beginners.

With all of these developments, it is important to acquire the necessary background knowledge of the fundamentals of cybersecurity. While it involves good technical knowledge, it is still possible even for a complete computer novice to gain a thorough understanding of the concepts and properties of cybersecurity and its prop.

The book is written in a way that is easy to understand. The technical concepts have been developed and explained in such a way that they will not be confusing for beginners.

CHAPTER 1

INTRODUCTION TO CYBERSPACE

Internet is the interconnected realm of digital systems, networks, and information, where individuals, businesses, and governments communicate, exchange data, and conduct various activities using electronic devices and the internet. It's a virtual environment that has become an integral part of modern society, shaping how we interact, learn, work, and entertain ourselves.

Internet is among the most important inventions of the 21 century which have affected our life. Today, Internet have crossed every barrier and have changed the way we used to talk, play games, workshop, make friends, listen to music, see movies, order food, pay bill, greet your friend on his birthday anniversary, etc., you name it. And we have an app in place for that. It has facilitated our life by making it comfortable. Gone are the days when we have to stand in a long queue for paying our telephone and electricity bills. Now we can pay it at a click of a button from our home or office, the technology have reached to an extent that we don't even require a computer for using Internet. Now we have Internet enabled smartphone TomTom's, et cetera, through which we can remain connected to our friends, family and office 24 by seven, not only Internet has simplified our life, but also it has brought many things within the reach of the middle class by making them cost effective.

It was not long back while making an IED or even an STD call, the eyes were stricken on the pulse meter the calls were very costly IED and were used to pass on urgent messages only and the rest of the routine communication was done using letters since it was a relatively very cheap.

Now, Internet have made it possible to not only talk, but use video conference using popular applications like Skype, G, talk, etc. at a very low price to a level where a one-hour video chat using Internet is cheaper.

Not only this Internet has changed, the use of the typical devices that were used by US television can be used not only for watching popular TV shows and movies, but can be used for calling video, chatting with friends, using Internet.

Mobile phone is not only used for making a call, but viewing a latest movie, we can remain connected to everyone no matter what our location is.

Working parents from office can keep an eye on their children at home and help them in their homework. A businessman can keep an eye on his staff office, shop, et cetera, with a click of a button. It has facilitated our life in more than one way. Have you ever wondered from where this Internet came, let us discuss the brief history of Internet and learn how this Internet was invented and how it evolved to an extent that now we cannot think of our lives without it.

In conclusion, internet has transformed the way we live, work, and interact, offering unprecedented opportunities for communication, innovation, and collaboration. However, as we embrace the benefits of this interconnected realm, it's important to be mindful of the challenges and security concerns it presents. Balancing the advantages with responsible online behavior and cybersecurity practices is essential for harnessing the full potential of cyberspace.

The History of Internet:

To know what the Cold War between USA and Russia gave to the world, but defiantly, the Internet is one of those very useful inventions whose foundation was laid during Cold War of nine days. Russia launched the world's first satellite, Sputnik, into the space on 4th October 1957. This was clearly the victory of Russia over the cyberspace and as a counter step, Advanced Research Projects Agency, the research arm of Department of Defense United States, declared the launch of ARPANET Advanced Research Projects Agency network in early 1960s. This was an experimental network and was designed to keep the computers connected to this network to communicate with each other, even if any of the node due to the bomb attack fails to respond. The first message was sent over the ARPANET, a packet switching network by Leonard Kleinrock Laboratory at University of California, Los Angeles, UCLA. You will be surprised to know that the first message that was sent over the Internet was lo actually. They intended to send work log in and only the first two letters reached its destination at Second Network Node at Stanford Research Institute Ezri. And before the last three letters could reach the destination, the network was down due to glitch. Soon the error was fixed and the message was resending it. The major test that ARPANET have to play is to develop rules for communication, i.e. protocols for communicating over ARPANET. The ARPANET in particular led to the development of protocols for internetworking, in which multiple separate networks could be joined into a network of networks. It resulted in the development of the protocol suite, which specifies the rules for joining and communicating over ARPANET. Soon after, in 1986, and as Foundational Science Foundation Backbone was created, two and five U.S. universities, computing centers were connected to Foremans fat. NSFNET, the successor of ARPANET, become popular by 1990 and ARPANET was decommissioned. There were many parallel networks developed by other universities and other countries like the United Kingdom. In 1965, National Physical Laboratory NGPL proposed a packing switching network, Michigan Educational Research Information Tribe formed former network in 1966, which was funded and supported by State of Michigan and the National Science Foundation NSF. France also developed a packet switching network no facilities in 1973.

Now, there were many parallel systems working on different protocols, and the scientists were looking for some common standard so that the networks could be interconnected.

In 1978, TCP IP protocol suits were ready and by 1983, the TCP IP protocol were adopted by ARPANET. In 1981, the integration of two large networks took place NAFS developed computer science networks CNN and was connected to ARPANET using TCP IP protocol suite. Now, the network was not only popular among the research community, but the private plane also took interest in the network. Initially, NAFS supported speed of 56 kilobits. It was upgraded to one point five megabits in 1988 to facilitate the growth of network by involving Merrett Network, IBM, MCI and the state of Michigan. After the Cafritz took realize the strength and merit of this network, they participated in the development of the network to reap its benefits. By late 1980s, many Internet service providers, ISPs emerged to provide the backbone for carrying the network traffic. By 1991, it was expended and was upgraded to 45 megabits per second. Many commercial ISPs provided backbone even as popular among the corporate, to facilitate the commercial use of the network. The Senate was decommissioned in 1995 and now the Internet could carry commercial traffic. So, this was the history of Internet where it came from.

Cybersecurity Models

In this section, we will learn about the CIA Triangle, Confidentiality, Integrity, and Availability, also known as the CIA Triangle, which is a security model created to guide security policies. confidentiality in an enterprise. The three elements of the CIA triangle of confidentiality, integrity, and availability are considered the three most important components of security. This information will be very useful if you work in the IT field or are planning to enter the field.

Confidentiality, confidentiality is the security principle that controls access to information. It is designed to ensure the wrong people cannot gain access to sensitive information while ensuring the right people can access it. Access to information must be restricted only to those who are authorized to view the required data.

Data can be categorized according to the type and severity of damage that could happen to it should it fall into unauthorized hands. According to these categories, strict measures can then be implemented. Protecting confidentiality may also include special training for those who share sensitive data, including familiarizing authorized users with security risk factors and teaching them how to guard vulnerable data assets. In addition to training, strong passwords and password related best practices must be used, as well as information about social engineering attacks to prevent them from unwittingly avoiding proper data handling rules and potentially causing disastrous results.

An example of a method used to ensure confidentiality is the use of data encryption to factor authentication is now becoming the norm for authenticating users to access sensitive data, while user IDs and passwords should be considered standard practice.

Other methods include biometric verification, security tokens and digital certificates, users should also be cautious to reduce the number of places where the information appears and where sensitive data is transmitted in order to complete a transaction. So, this was all about confidentiality. In the next section, we are going to learn what is integrity.

Integrity, the second component of the triad integrity this assures the sensitive data is trustworthy and accurate. Consistency, accuracy and trustworthiness of data should be maintained over its lifecycle. Sensitive data should not be altered in transit and security measures such as file permissions and user access controls should be taken to make sure that it cannot be modified by unauthorized users.

In addition, version control should be used to prevent unintentional changes and deletions from authorized users from becoming a problem.

Other measures should also be taken to detect data changes that might occur due to a non-human caused event such as a server crash or an environmental failure. Sensitive data should also include cryptographic checksums for verification of integrity.

In addition, backups for redundancy plans should be planned and implemented to restore any affected data in case of an integrity failure or security breach in order to restore data back to its correct state.

Availability is the guarantee of reliable and constant access to your sensitive data by authorized people, it is best guaranteed by properly maintaining all hardware and software necessary to ensure the availability of sensitive data. It's also important to keep up with system upgrades. Providing adequate communication, throughput and preventing bottleneck helps as well. Redundancy, failover, rate and clustering are important measures that should be considered to avoid serious availability problems. A quick adaptive disaster recovery plan is crucial for the worst-case scenarios, which will depend on the successful execution of a full disaster recovery plan. Safeguards against interruptions and connections and data loss should consider unpredictable events such as a fire or a natural disaster to prevent data loss, backup should be located in a geographically separate location and in a fireproof waterproof vault to prevent downtime due to malicious attacks, such as denial of service attacks and network intrusions. Extra software and security equipment should be used as well. So, this was all about CIA trained. Conclusion of this section is the CIA security triangle is an important security concept because all security controls, mechanisms and safeguards are implemented to provide one or more of these protection types. All risks, threats and vulnerabilities are measured for their potential capability to compromise one or all of the CIA triad principles. This triad is the basis for creating a holistic security plan to protect all of your organization's critical and sensitive assets.

A cybersecurity model is a structured framework or approach that organizations and individuals use to manage and enhance their cybersecurity posture. It provides a systematic way to identify, assess, protect, detect, respond to, and recover from cyber threats and attacks. Here's an overview of a commonly used cybersecurity model:

NIST Cybersecurity Framework:

The National Institute of Standards and Technology (NIST) Cybersecurity Framework is a widely adopted model that offers guidelines for improving cybersecurity across critical infrastructure sectors. It consists of five key functions:

Identify: Understand and manage cybersecurity risks to systems, assets, data, and capabilities. This involves:

- Asset Management: Identifying and categorizing critical assets.
- Risk Assessment: Evaluating vulnerabilities and potential impacts.
- Governance: Establishing cybersecurity policies and responsibilities.

Protect: Implement safeguards to limit or contain the impact of potential cyber threats. This includes:

- Access Control: Restricting unauthorized access to systems and data.
- Data Security: Encrypting sensitive information to ensure confidentiality.
- Awareness Training: Educating employees about security best practices.

Detect: Implement measures to identify cybersecurity events promptly. This involves:

- Continuous Monitoring: Monitoring networks and systems for suspicious activities.
- Intrusion Detection: Identifying unauthorized access attempts or breaches.
- Incident Detection: Recognizing and reporting potential security incidents.

Respond: Develop and implement an effective response plan to address detected cybersecurity incidents. This includes:

- Incident Response Plan: Outlining steps to take in case of a breach.
- Communication: Informing stakeholders about the incident and its impact.
- Containment: Isolating affected systems to prevent further damage.

Recover: Develop and implement strategies for restoring normal operations after a cybersecurity incident. This involves:

- Data Recovery: Restoring lost or compromised data from backups.
- Business Continuity: Ensuring essential services can resume despite disruptions.
- Lessons Learned: Analyzing the incident to improve future response and prevention.

Adopting the NIST Framework:

Organizations can customize the NIST framework to their specific needs and size. They can assess their current cybersecurity posture, identify gaps, and develop a roadmap for improvement. The framework promotes a risk-based approach, where security measures are aligned with the organization's risk tolerance and business objectives.

By following a cybersecurity model like the NIST Cybersecurity Framework, organizations can establish a comprehensive and effective cybersecurity strategy. Regular assessments, updates, and collaboration with stakeholder's help ensure that security measures remain effective in an ever-evolving threat landscape.

FARHADUR RAHIM

The Core Cyber Attacks

Welcome to this new section on cybercrime where we will learn different types of cybercrime. The Internet was born around 1966, when its access was limited to a few scientific researchers and the defense only Internet user base have evolved exponentially.

In the beginning, computer crime was limited to damaging computers and infrastructure.

Around 1980, did the trend change from physically damaging computers to causing computers to malfunction using malicious code called viruses?

Until then, this effect was not so widespread as the Internet was limited to large international companies and defense configuration research communities.

In 1996, when the Internet came out to the public, it immediately became popular among the masses and they gradually became addicted to it as it changed their way of life. Good things are so well written that users don't have to worry about how the internet works, they just make you click on hyperlinks or type the desired information where you want it without worrying about Where and how is this data stored. sent over the Internet, or whether data can be viewed by another person connected to the Internet, or whether data packets sent over the Internet can be collected and censored.

The goals of computer crime have changed from just damaging computers or destroying or manipulating data for personal gain to financial crimes.

These computer attacks are multiplying at a rapid rate. Every second about 25 computers are victims of cyberattacks and around 800 million people are affected as of 2013. It is also estimated that around $160 million is lost each year to cybercrime. This number is very cautious because most cases are never reported. Before we dig deeper, let us know what cybercrime is.

The term cybercrime is used to describe an illegal activity in which a computer or computing device such as a smartphone, tablet, personal digital assistant, Pedder, etc., is autonomous. or as part of a network, used as a tool or slash and target of criminal activity. It is often done by people with a destructive and criminal mindset, whether for revenge, greed, or adventure.

Now let's see the main two types of cybercrime.

Cybercriminals can be internal or external to the organization facing a cyber-attack, based on this fact, cybercriminals can be classified into two types of internal attacks and external attacks. Now, in this particular lecture, we are going to talk about insider attacks. This is an attack on a computer network or system by someone with authorized access to the system, known as an insider attack. It is usually done by unhappy or disgruntled employees or contractors. The motive of insider attack can be revenge or greed, it is relatively easy for insiders to perform a cyber-attack because they are familiar with IT policies, procedures, and processes. architecture and stability of the security system.

In addition, the attacker has access to the network, so it is relatively easy for an internal attacker to steal sensitive information, browse the network, etc.

In most cases, the reason for an insider attack is when an employee is terminated or assigned a new role within an organization and that role is not reflected in IT policy. This opens a vulnerability window for the attacker.

Insider attacks can be avoided by planning and installing an internal intrusion detection system in an organization, these attacks can be very dangerous because the attackers are inside the network. Therefore, it was an insider attack.

Now, let's learn about the external attack, which is the opposite of the inside attack. When an attacker is hired by an insider or entity outside the organization, it is an external attack. An organization that is the victim of a cyber-attack suffers not only financial loss but also reputational loss because the attacker is someone outside the organization. As a result, these attackers often analyze and gather information and display and network security administrators keep logs generated by firewalls, because external attacks can be tracked by carefully analyze these firewall logs. In addition, intrusion detection systems are installed to monitor external attacks. External attacks are usually carried out by black hat hackers, don't worry if you don't know about them, I will tell you about the types of hackers we have in the next section. External attacks are always carried out with the aim of obtaining unauthorized data and obtaining financial gain.

Exploring the Various Types of Cybercrime by Terms

In today's digitized world, the rapid advancement of technology has brought unprecedented convenience and connectivity. However, it has also ushered in a new era of criminal activity: cybercrime. From individuals to corporations and governments, no entity is immune to the threats posed by these virtual criminals. This section delves into the various types of cybercrime, shedding light on the diverse tactics employed by cybercriminals.

Phishing:

One of the most prevalent forms of cybercrime is phishing. Cybercriminals send deceptive emails, messages, or websites that mimic legitimate entities, aiming to trick recipients into divulging sensitive information, such as passwords, credit card details, or personal identification. Phishing attacks prey on human psychology, often relying on urgency or authority to manipulate victims.

Malware Attacks:

Malicious software, or malware, is a versatile tool in the hands of cybercriminals. It encompasses viruses, worms, trojans, ransomware, and spyware. These programs are designed to infiltrate computer systems, steal data, or disrupt operations. Ransomware, for instance, encrypts a victim's data and demands a ransom for its release, causing financial loss and operational chaos.

Identity Theft:

Stealing personal information for financial gain is the hallmark of identity theft. Cybercriminals acquire sensitive data, such as social security numbers, bank details, and medical records, to commit fraudulent activities like opening accounts, making purchases, or even committing more serious crimes in the victim's name.

Cyberbullying and Harassment:
The digital world has provided a platform for cyberbullies and harassers to target individuals with hurtful messages, threats, or false accusations. Social media platforms, messaging apps, and online forums become arenas for these malicious activities, often leading to emotional distress and psychological harm.

Online Scams:
Cybercriminals frequently design elaborate scams to exploit individuals' trust or lack of knowledge. These scams can take various forms, such as lottery frauds, fake charity appeals, or investment schemes promising unrealistic returns. Victims are manipulated into parting with their money or personal information.

Cyber Espionage:
Cybercriminals sponsored by governments, organizations, or nation-states engage in cyber espionage to steal sensitive information or intellectual property from other governments, corporations, or individuals. The stolen data could include trade secrets, research, military intelligence, or strategic plans.

Data Breaches:
Data breaches involve unauthorized access to an organization's or individual's data, leading to its exposure or theft. These breaches often result from inadequate security measures or vulnerabilities in systems. Stolen data can be sold on the dark web or used for identity theft and financial fraud.

Hacking:
Hacking refers to unauthorized access to computer systems or networks. Hackers exploit security vulnerabilities to gain control, steal data, or disrupt operations. They can be motivated by financial gain, political activism, or personal vendettas.

Cyberstalking:

Similar to traditional stalking, cyberstalking involves unwanted, persistent online attention that causes fear or distress to the victim. The anonymity and ease of communication online make cyberstalking a concerning issue, often involving threats, monitoring, or invasive messages.

Child Exploitation:

The dark side of the internet also includes crimes against children. Cybercriminals may engage in child pornography, grooming, or luring minors into unsafe situations. Law enforcement agencies worldwide collaborate to combat these heinous acts.

In conclusion, the landscape of cybercrime is vast and continually evolving. From phishing attacks to child exploitation, cybercriminals employ diverse tactics to exploit vulnerabilities and cause harm. As individuals, businesses, and governments strive to adapt to the digital age, it is crucial to remain vigilant, adopt robust cybersecurity measures, and stay informed about the ever-changing methods of cybercriminals. Only by working together can we hope to mitigate the risks and create a safer online environment for everyone.

Techniques and Motivations Behind Cyber Attacks

Exploiting Vulnerabilities:
Attackers identify and exploit weaknesses in software, networks, or human behavior to gain unauthorized access.

Zero-Day Exploits:
Exploiting undisclosed vulnerabilities before software vendors can issue patches.

Economic Motivations:
Many attacks are financially driven, seeking monetary gain through data theft, ransom payments, or fraudulent activities.

Espionage and Cyber Warfare:
Nation-states engage in cyber-attacks for political, strategic, or intelligence-gathering purposes.

Hacktivism:
Ideologically motivated attacks seek to promote a cause, often with political or social underpinnings.

The Impact of Cyber Attacks: Unraveling the Digital Disruption

In the interconnected landscape of the digital age, the rapid evolution of technology has brought unprecedented convenience and efficiency to our lives. However, it has also given rise to a new breed of threats: cyber-attacks. These malicious acts, carried out in the virtual realm, have the potential to disrupt, damage, or compromise various aspects of modern society, from individual privacy to critical infrastructure. In this section, we delve deep into the intricate web of the impact of cyber-attacks, exploring their ramifications across different sectors and offering insights into mitigation strategies.

1. Financial Fallout:

One of the most immediate and tangible consequences of cyber-attacks is financial losses. From small businesses to multinational corporations, these attacks can lead to substantial monetary damages. Data breaches expose sensitive information, including personal details and financial records, leading to potential legal action, hefty fines, and compensation claims. Additionally, the cost of mitigating the attack, restoring systems, and implementing cybersecurity measures can strain budgets and impact profitability.

2. Disruption of Operations:

Cyber-attacks have the power to bring organizations to a standstill by disrupting operations, often resulting in substantial downtimes. Ransomware attacks, for instance, can lock vital systems and data, rendering them inaccessible until a ransom is paid. The ripple effects of these disruptions extend beyond immediate financial losses, affecting customer trust, employee productivity, and overall business continuity.

3. Erosion of Trust:

The aftermath of a cyber-attack extends beyond the immediate financial impact. Organizations that fall victim to attacks can suffer reputational damage, eroding the trust of customers, partners, and stakeholders. Public perception of a brand's security measures significantly influences consumer decisions. A breach of customer data not only leads to a loss of trust but can also result in long-term customer attrition.

4. National Security Concerns:

Beyond the corporate world, cyber-attacks pose significant national security concerns. Nation-states and political actors often engage in cyber warfare, targeting critical infrastructure, government systems, and sensitive data. These attacks can disrupt essential services, undermine public safety, and compromise national security strategies. The potential consequences of cyber-attacks on national security underscore the importance of robust cybersecurity measures and international cooperation.

5. Intellectual Property Theft:

In the realm of innovation and creativity, cyber-attacks can result in the theft of intellectual property, trade secrets, and proprietary information. This not only impacts the organization's competitive advantage but also stifles innovation as stolen ideas are exploited by unauthorized entities.

6. Psychological and Emotional Toll:

Individuals who fall victim to cyber-attacks, such as online harassment, identity theft, or data breaches, can experience psychological and emotional distress. The invasion of privacy, violation of personal space, and fear of potential repercussions can lead to anxiety, stress, and long-lasting emotional trauma.

The Significance of Cybersecurity: Safeguarding the Digital Realm

In an age defined by digital innovation and interconnectedness, the importance of cybersecurity cannot be overstated. As our lives become increasingly intertwined with technology, the protection of digital assets, personal information, and critical infrastructure has emerged as a paramount concern. This section delves into the compelling reasons why cybersecurity holds such a vital place in our modern world.

Protection of Sensitive Data:

Our digital lives are filled with sensitive information, ranging from personal identification details to financial records and medical histories. Cybersecurity measures ensure that this information remains confidential and secure, shielding individuals from identity theft, fraud, and other malicious activities.

Preservation of Privacy:

The digital landscape can often feel like an open book, with every online interaction leaving a trace. Cybersecurity helps preserve our right to privacy by safeguarding our personal communications, online behavior, and interactions from unauthorized access or surveillance.

Prevention of Financial Loss:

Cybercriminals target financial institutions, e-commerce platforms, and individuals to steal money or gain unauthorized access to accounts. Effective cybersecurity measures protect individuals and organizations from losing substantial sums of money through fraudulent activities like phishing, ransomware attacks, and online scams.

Defending Against Cybercrime:

The rise of cybercrime has led to a surge in various malicious activities, including hacking, data breaches, and online fraud. Robust cybersecurity practices act as a bulwark against these threats, thwarting cybercriminal's attempts to compromise systems, steal data, and wreak havoc.

Ensuring Business Continuity:

For businesses, a cyberattack can result in devastating financial losses, damage to reputation, and even closure. Implementing cybersecurity measures safeguards business operations, customer trust, and intellectual property, ensuring uninterrupted services and smooth operations.

Protecting National Security:

Cyberattacks on critical infrastructure, government systems, and military networks can have far-reaching implications for national security. Strong cybersecurity defenses prevent hostile actors from compromising essential services and sensitive information that could jeopardize a nation's security and stability.

Preserving Digital Trust:

In an era dominated by digital interactions, trust is paramount. Cybersecurity instills confidence among individuals, businesses, and governments, fostering a sense of security and encouraging participation in online activities without fear of data breaches or unauthorized access.

Facilitating Innovation:

As technology evolves, so do cyber threats. Effective cybersecurity practices enable organizations to embrace innovation without fear of jeopardizing their digital assets or intellectual property. This, in turn, encourages ongoing technological advancements.

Mitigating Legal and Regulatory Risks

In many jurisdictions, organizations are legally obligated to protect sensitive customer data. Failing to implement adequate cybersecurity measures can result in severe legal consequences, fines, and reputational damage.

Promoting Digital Resilience:

As cyber threats become more sophisticated, organizations must develop resilience to withstand attacks. Cybersecurity strategies encompass risk assessment, incident response planning, and proactive defense mechanisms that allow organizations to recover swiftly from any breach.

Robust Cybersecurity Measures: Implement advanced security protocols, firewalls, and intrusion detection systems to prevent unauthorized access and mitigate risks.

Education and Training: Equip employees, users, and stakeholders with cybersecurity knowledge to recognize and respond to potential threats.

Incident Response Plans: Develop comprehensive incident response plans that outline steps to take when a cyber-attack occurs, facilitating swift and effective recovery.

Regular Updates and Patches: Keep software, operating systems, and applications up to date to address vulnerabilities and prevent exploitation.

Collaboration and Information Sharing: Foster collaboration between public and private sectors to share threat intelligence and develop strategies for collective defense.

In a world where technology interweaves with every facet of our lives, the impact of cyber-attacks is far-reaching and complex. As the threat landscape evolves, so must our defenses. By understanding the potential consequences of cyber-attacks and adopting proactive measures, we can collectively safeguard our digital ecosystem and preserve the benefits of the interconnected world we live in.

In conclusion, the importance of cybersecurity resonates throughout our digital lives, touching every facet of society. From individual privacy to national security, from financial stability to innovation, cybersecurity plays a pivotal role in ensuring the continued growth and prosperity of our interconnected world. By staying vigilant, adopting best practices, and prioritizing cybersecurity, individuals, businesses, and governments can collectively create a safer digital landscape for all.

CHAPTER 2

HACKER AND THEIR JOBS

In the ever-evolving realm of technology and the digital landscape, hackers have become both enigmatic figures and influential actors. Often depicted in pop culture as shadowy individuals tapping away at keyboards, the reality of hackers and their roles is more nuanced. This introduction provides insight into the world of hackers, exploring their motivations, classifications, and various roles they play in the digital ecosystem.

The term "hacker" carries a spectrum of meanings, largely dependent on the context in which it is used. At its core, a hacker is an individual who possesses advanced computer skills and knowledge, enabling them to manipulate and access computer systems, networks, and software beyond conventional usage. Contrary to popular belief, not all hackers engage in malicious activities; there are distinct categories that highlight diverse motivations and intentions.

What is a Hacker

Hacking involves identifying weaknesses in a computer system or network to exploit those weaknesses to gain access to them, e.g. attack using password cracking algorithms to gain access to the system. Computers have become imperative to run a successful business, it is not enough to have isolated computer systems, they must be networked to facilitate communication with outside companies. This exposes them to the outside world and gets hacked. Hacking means using a computer to perform fraudulent acts such as fraud, privacy, intrusion, theft, company personal data, etc. Cybercrime costs many organizations millions of dollars each year, businesses need to protect themselves against such attacks. A hacker is someone who is extremely interested in the mysterious workings of any computer operating system. Hackers are usually programmers. They gain advanced knowledge of operating systems and programming languages, and discover loopholes within systems and their causes. Who is a hacker and the types of hackers? Hackers are people who find and exploit weaknesses in computer systems and/or networks to gain access, hackers are usually skilled computer programmers with knowledge of computer security.

There we have three types of hackers. White hat, black hat and gray hat, we will talk about each.

Classified or Categories of Hackers

The first one on our list is Black Hat Hacker. So now let's learn and know who are black hat hackers.

Black Hat Hackers:

The term black originated from western movies where the bad guys wire black hats and the good guys wire white hats, black hat, hackers, an individual who attempts to gain unauthorized entry into a system or network to exploit them for malicious reasons. The Black Hat hacker does not have any permission or authority to compromise their targets. They try to inflict damage by compromising security systems, altering the functions of websites and networks, or shutting down systems. They often do so to steal or gain access to passwords, financial information, and other personal data. Black hat hackers are illegal because they are used to perform criminal activities like hacking accounts, stealing data, financial theft, blackmailing, and many more. All these illegal activities are performed by them black hat hackers are not authorized hackers, they are not having any kind of permission from the admin to hack them. I will always prefer if you want to become a hacker, please choose the path of ethical hacking, do not go on the path of black hat hackers.

White Hat Hacker:

On the other hand, white hat hackers are considered good people who work with organizations to increase the security of the system. A white hat hacker has the power to interact with targets and compromise them according to the prescribed rules of interaction. White hat hackers are often referred to as ethical hackers. This person specializes in ethical hacking tools, techniques, and methods for securing an organization's information systems. Unlike black hat hackers, ethical hackers exploit secure networks and look for backdoors when they are legally allowed to do so. White hat hackers always disclose any vulnerabilities they find in the company's security systems so that they can be patched before they are exploited by malicious actors. Some Fortune 50 companies like Facebook, Microsoft and Google also use hackers, so these are good companies. They have admin rights and permission to perform penetration testing. If you want to be an ethical hacker choose this ethical hacking path, ethical hacking is a great profession to pursue today. The demand for ethical hackers is growing and the supply is not so good. So, this is a very good opportunity to learn about cyber security and hacking and get the desired job.

Grey Hat Hackers:

Now, let's see who are grey hat hackers, Gray hat hackers, exploit networks and computer systems in the way that black hats do, but do so without any malicious intent, disclosing all loopholes and vulnerabilities to law enforcement agencies or intelligence agencies.

Usually, grey hat hackers surf the Net and hack into computer systems to notify the administrator or the owner that their systems network contains one or more vulnerabilities that must be fixed immediately.

Gray hats may also extort the hacked offering to correct the defect for a nominal fee. Basically, grey hat hackers are a mixture of black hat hackers and white hat hackers. So, this was all about a grey hat hacker.

Hacktivists:

They are driven by political, social, or ideological motivations. They use hacking skills to promote a cause, raise awareness, or challenge systems they perceive as unjust. Their actions can range from website defacements to releasing sensitive information.

Script Kiddies:

These hackers lack deep technical knowledge and often rely on existing tools and scripts to carry out attacks. While their actions may be less sophisticated, they can still cause disruptions and damage.

Roles of Hackers: Navigating the Digital Landscape

Security Experts: Ethical hackers and security professionals are instrumental in identifying vulnerabilities and fortifying systems against cyber threats. They work to prevent breaches and protect sensitive data.

Bug Bounty Hunters: These hackers participate in bug bounty programs, which organizations run to encourage cybersecurity researchers to find and report vulnerabilities. In exchange for responsibly disclosing security flaws, bug bounty hunters receive rewards, fostering a cooperative approach to improving security.

Penetration Testers: Often hired by organizations, penetration testers simulate cyberattacks to assess the effectiveness of security measures. Their findings help organizations improve their defenses.

Cybersecurity Researchers: Hackers contribute to

cybersecurity research by uncovering new vulnerabilities, developing patches, and sharing knowledge to enhance overall security.

Innovators: Some hackers are innovators who contribute to the development of new tools, technologies, and solutions that benefit both security professionals and the general public.

Threat Actors: Malicious hackers, including cybercriminals and state-sponsored actors, target individuals, organizations, and even governments with the intent to steal data, disrupt operations, or compromise security.

Malware Analysts: They dissect malicious software to understand its functionality, behavior, and potential impact. Their insights contribute to developing strategies to detect, mitigate, and prevent malware infections.

In conclusion, hackers occupy a diverse landscape, ranging from those who work tirelessly to fortify digital defenses to those who exploit vulnerabilities for personal gain or ideological reasons. The roles they play in the digital realm have far-reaching implications, shaping the cybersecurity landscape and our understanding of technology's impact on society. As technology evolves, so too do the roles of hackers, underscoring the need for vigilance, ethical responsibility, and continuous innovation in the world of cybersecurity.

Understanding Crackers:

Crackers are individuals who engage in unauthorized activities with malicious intent, such as breaking into systems, stealing data, and causing harm.

Intent: Crackers are typically driven by personal gain, financial motives, or disruption of services.

Characteristics:

- Crackers often operate outside the boundaries of law and ethics, engaging in cybercrime for financial or personal gain.
- Their activities can include data breaches, identity theft, cyberattacks, and other harmful actions.
- Crackers exploit vulnerabilities in systems to compromise security and access sensitive information.

Key Differences:

Intent: The primary difference between hackers and crackers lies in their intent. Hackers may engage in activities for various purposes, including ethical ones, while crackers are motivated by malicious goals.

Ethics: Hackers can be ethical or unethical, depending on their actions. Crackers, by definition, engage in activities that violate ethical and legal standards.

Actions: Hackers may work to improve security, innovate, or expose vulnerabilities for the greater good. Crackers, on the other hand, seek personal gain or engage in cybercriminal activities.

Impact: Hackers can have positive impacts on cybersecurity by identifying vulnerabilities and helping organizations improve their defenses. Crackers, on the other hand, have negative impacts through their malicious activities.

In conclusion, understanding the distinctions between hackers and crackers is essential for a comprehensive understanding of the digital landscape. While hackers encompass a wide range of roles, motivations, and actions, crackers are specifically associated with malicious and unauthorized activities. By recognizing these differences, individuals can better navigate the complexities of cybersecurity and the various actors within the digital realm.

CHAPTER 3

OVERVIEW MALWARE

The history of malware (malicious software) traces back to the early days of computing, and it has evolved significantly over the decades. Malware refers to software specifically designed to infiltrate, damage, or gain unauthorized access to computer systems and networks. Here's a brief overview of its history:

1960s and 1970s - The Birth of Malicious Code:

The earliest forms of malware were not as complex as modern examples. One of the first recorded instances was the Creeper virus in the 1970s, which spread across ARPANET (an early precursor to the internet) and displayed a simple message. The Reaper program was created in response to remove Creeper, making it somewhat of a precursor to antivirus solutions.

1980s - The Rise of Viruses:

The 1980s saw the emergence of more sophisticated malware. The concept of computer viruses gained prominence with the release of the Elk Cloner in 1982, which targeted Apple II computers. The Brain virus, released in 1986, was the first IBM PC-compatible virus. Viruses like these were often spread through infected floppy disks.

1990s - Worms and Internet Era:

The 1990s brought about the era of worms, which are self-replicating malware that spread over networks. The Morris Worm, created in 1988, was one of the first instances of worms causing significant damage. The 1990s also witnessed the rise of Trojans (malware disguised as legitimate software), and macro viruses spread through documents.

2000s - Commercialization and Advanced Malware:

The 2000s marked a period of increased commercialization of malware. Malware authors started creating malware for financial gain, stealing personal information, and carrying out targeted attacks. The ILOVEYOU worm, distributed via email in 2000, was one of the most widespread viruses. This decade also saw the emergence of ransomware, which encrypts users' data and demands a ransom for its release.

2010s - A New Level of Sophistication:

The 2010s saw a significant increase in the sophistication of malware. Advanced Persistent Threats (APTs) gained attention, with state-sponsored actors creating targeted and highly advanced malware for espionage and cyber warfare.

Stuxnet, discovered in 2010, was a famous example of a state-sponsored worm targeting industrial systems.

Modern Times - Diverse Threat Landscape:

The present era features a diverse range of malware types, including ransomware, banking Trojans, spyware, and mobile malware. Ransomware attacks like WannaCry and NotPetya garnered global attention due to their wide-reaching impacts.

Ongoing Evolution:

Malware continues to evolve with emerging technologies. The rise of IoT (Internet of Things) devices presents new attack vectors, and techniques like fileless malware and polymorphic malware make detection and prevention more challenging.

To counter the growing threat, cybersecurity measures have also advanced. Antivirus software, intrusion detection systems, firewalls, and advanced threat detection technologies are employed to mitigate the risks posed by malware. However, as malware continues to evolve, the battle between cybercriminals and security professionals remains ongoing.

Types of Malware:

Certainly, here are some of the most common types of malware:

Viruses:

Viruses are pieces of code that attach themselves to legitimate programs or files and replicate when the infected program is executed. They can spread throughout a system, often leading to data corruption or destruction.

Worms:

Worms are self-replicating malware that spread over networks without needing to attach to other programs. They exploit vulnerabilities in network protocols to infect and propagate themselves to other devices.

Trojans:

Trojans, named after the Greek myth of the Trojan Horse, are malware that disguises itself as legitimate software. Once executed, they can perform a range of malicious activities, such as stealing sensitive information, providing unauthorized access, or opening backdoors for other malware.

Ransomware:

Ransomware encrypts the victim's data and demands a ransom in exchange for the decryption key. It can cause significant disruption to individuals and organizations by rendering their files inaccessible until the ransom is paid.

FARHADUR RAHIM

Spyware:

Spyware is designed to gather sensitive information from a device without the user's consent. This can include keystrokes, browsing habits, login credentials, and more. The collected data is usually sent to a remote attacker.

Adware:

Adware displays unwanted advertisements to users. While not inherently malicious, adware can be annoying and negatively impact system performance. Some adware may also collect user data to target ads more effectively.

Keyloggers:

Keyloggers record keystrokes made on a compromised system, allowing attackers to capture sensitive information like usernames, passwords, and credit card details.

Rootkits:

Rootkits are designed to hide malicious software or processes from detection by operating systems and security software. They often gain elevated privileges, enabling them to control the compromised system at a deep level.

Botnets:

Botnets are networks of infected computers (known as bots) that are controlled remotely by a central server. They can be used to launch coordinated attacks, distribute spam, or carry out other malicious activities.

Backdoors:

Backdoors are secret access points left by attackers in a system, providing them with ongoing access without the user's knowledge. They can be used to return to the compromised system even after initial removal of malware.

Fileless Malware:

Fileless malware resides in a computer's memory and doesn't leave a footprint on the disk, making it harder to detect and remove. It often exploits legitimate tools and processes to carry out malicious activities.

Mobile Malware:

Mobile devices are not immune to malware. Mobile malware can include various types like banking Trojans, spyware, and adware, targeting smartphones and tablets.

These are just a few examples of the many types of malware that exist. As technology evolves, cybercriminals continue to develop new and more sophisticated malware variants, making effective cybersecurity measures an ongoing challenge.

The Purpose of Malware

Malware is used for a variety of malicious purposes, often driven by financial gain, espionage, disruption, or simply the intent to cause harm. Here are some common reasons why malware is used:

Financial Gain:

Many cybercriminals create and deploy malware with the primary goal of making money. This can involve stealing personal and financial information, conducting online fraud, or launching ransomware attacks that demand payment for the release of encrypted data.

Data Theft:

Malware can be used to steal sensitive information such as credit card numbers, login credentials, personal identities, and proprietary business data. Stolen data can be sold on the black market or used for identity theft.

Espionage and Surveillance:

State-sponsored actors, intelligence agencies, and corporate competitors may use malware to gain unauthorized access to computer systems and networks. This allows them to monitor communications, gather sensitive information, and gain a competitive advantage.

Disruption and Sabotage:

Some malware is designed to disrupt the operations of organizations or governments. This can involve targeting critical infrastructure, such as power grids or transportation systems, to cause chaos and disruption.

Extortion and Ransomware:

Ransomware is a form of malware that encrypts a victim's data and demands payment (a ransom) for the decryption key. Cybercriminals use this method to extort money from individuals, businesses, and even governmental entities.

Botnets and DDoS Attacks:

Malware can be used to create botnets—networks of infected computers under the control of an attacker. These botnets can be used to launch Distributed Denial of Service (DDoS) attacks, overwhelming websites or online services with traffic and causing them to become inaccessible.

State-Sponsored Cyber Operations:

Some countries develop and deploy malware for cyber espionage, information warfare, and geopolitical purposes. These operations can involve gathering intelligence, disrupting adversaries' infrastructure, or launching offensive cyber-attacks.

Political and Ideological Motivations:

Hacktivists and groups with political or ideological agendas may use malware to promote their causes. This can involve defacing websites, leaking sensitive data, or disrupting online platforms.

Testing and Research:

Ethical hackers, security researchers, and penetration testers may use malware in controlled environments to identify vulnerabilities and weaknesses in computer systems and networks. This helps organizations improve their security measures.

It's important to note that while some instances of malware are created with specific goals in mind, the proliferation of malware has led to unintended consequences, such as the widespread disruption of critical services and financial losses for individuals and organizations. As technology advances, understanding and countering the motivations behind malware usage remain essential for maintaining a secure online environment.

How Malware Works?

Certainly, let's delve into how malware works in more detail. Malware, short for malicious software, encompasses a wide range of software designed to perform malicious actions on computer systems, networks, and devices. The way malware works can vary based on its type and intended purpose. Here's an overview of how malware operates:

Infection and Delivery:

Malware typically enters a system through various vectors, including infected email attachments, malicious websites, compromised software, or infected removable media (such as USB drives). Users unknowingly interact with these vectors, initiating the malware's delivery onto their systems.

Execution:

Once inside the system, the malware needs to execute. This can happen through user interaction (e.g., opening an infected email attachment) or exploiting vulnerabilities in the system or software (e.g., exploiting a security flaw in an outdated application).

Establishing Persistence:

Many types of malware aim to maintain their presence on the infected system. They do this by creating registry entries, modifying system files, or utilizing rootkit techniques to hide their presence from security software.

Propagation and Spreading:

Some malware, like worms, are designed to self-replicate and spread across networks or to other devices. They achieve this by exploiting network vulnerabilities, infecting connected devices, and creating additional entry points for other malware.

Contacting Command and Control (C&C) Servers:

To receive instructions or updates, many types of malware establish connections to remote servers operated by attackers. These servers are known as Command and Control (C&C) servers. Malware can receive commands, upload stolen data, and download additional malicious payloads from these servers.

Data Theft or Surveillance:

Many malware types, such as spyware and keyloggers, aim to steal sensitive information. They capture keystrokes, record screen activity, and exfiltrate data to remote servers controlled by attackers. This stolen data can then be exploited for various purposes, including identity theft and financial fraud.

Ransomware Encryption:

Ransomware encrypts files on the victim's system, making them inaccessible until a ransom is paid for the decryption key. Ransomware often displays a ransom note demanding payment in cryptocurrency to release the encrypted data.

Botnet Formation:

Some malware, like botnets, aims to create networks of compromised devices under the control of a central attacker. These networks can be used for various purposes, such as launching DDoS attacks, sending spam, or mining cryptocurrency.

Exploiting Vulnerabilities:

Malware often takes advantage of software vulnerabilities to gain access to a system. This could involve exploiting flaws in operating systems, applications, or even browser plugins.

Evading Detection:

Many malware variants use techniques to evade detection by security software. This can include obfuscating their code, using encryption to hide communication, and employing polymorphic techniques that change their appearance with each infection.

Updating and Evolving:

Attackers continuously update and evolve malware to counteract security measures and to take advantage of new vulnerabilities. This ongoing development helps them maintain their ability to compromise systems.

To protect against malware, users and organizations should practice good cybersecurity hygiene, such as keeping software updated, using strong passwords, employing reputable security software, and being cautious when interacting with emails and websites.

Difference between Malware and Virus

Malware and viruses are related terms, but they refer to different concepts in the realm of cybersecurity. Here's the difference between malware and viruses:

Malware:

"Malware" is a broad term that stands for "malicious software." It encompasses all types of malicious software programs designed to harm, compromise, or gain unauthorized access to computer systems, networks, and devices. Malware is an umbrella term that includes various categories of malicious software, such as viruses, worms, Trojans, ransomware, spyware, adware, and more.

In other words, malware is the overarching term that covers all forms of harmful software, regardless of their specific behaviors or mechanisms.

Virus:

A "virus" is a specific type of malware. It is a self-replicating program that attaches itself to legitimate files or programs and spreads by infecting other files or programs. Viruses require human action to execute and spread. They typically attach themselves to executable files or documents, and when those files are opened or executed, the virus code is activated, and it can replicate and infect other files on the same system.

Key characteristics of viruses include:

Replication: Viruses are capable of self-replication by attaching themselves to other files.

Human Action: Viruses require a user to execute an infected file or program to initiate the infection.

Infection Mechanism: They attach their code to legitimate files, which helps them spread to other files or systems.

Need for Host Files: Viruses cannot function independently and rely on host files to carry their code.

In summary, while **"malware"** is a general term encompassing all types of malicious software, a **"virus"** is a specific category of malware that spreads by infecting other files and relies on human interaction to activate its malicious code.

CHAPTER 4

UNDERSTANDING CYBERCRIMES

Cybercrime is experiencing tremendous growth in today's technology world. World Wide Web criminals exploit the personal information of Internet users for their own profit. They go deep into the dark web to buy and sell illegal products and services. They even have access to classified government information. Cybercrime is at an unprecedented rate and costs businesses and individuals billions of dollars each year. What's even more frightening is that this number only represents the last 5 years without end. The evolution of technology and the increasing accessibility of smart technology mean that there are more access points to users' homes that hackers can exploit. As law enforcement tries to tackle this growing problem, the number of criminals continues to grow, taking advantage of the anonymity of the Internet.

we are getting to know what is cybercrime and their impact. So, let's get started.

What is Cybercrime?

Cybercrime also called computer crime, the use of a computer as an instrument to further illegal ends, such as committing fraud, trafficking in child pornography and intellectual property, stealing identities or violating privacy. Cybercrime, especially through the Internet, has grown in importance as the computer has become central to commerce, entertainment and government. Because of the early and widespread adoption of computers and the Internet in the United States, most of the earliest victims and villains of cybercrime were Americans. By the 21st century, though, partly Hamlet remained anywhere in the world that had not been touched by cybercrime of one sort or another. New technologies create new criminal opportunities, but few new types of crime.

Distinguishes between cybercrime and traditional criminal activity?

Obviously, one difference is the use of the digital computer. But technology alone is insufficient for any distinction that might exist between different realms of criminal activity. Criminals do not need a computer to commit fraud, trafficking, child pornography and intellectual property, steal an identity or violate someone's privacy. All those activities existed before the cyber prefix became ubiquitous. Cybercrime, especially involving the Internet, represents an extension of existing criminal behavior alongside some novel illegal activities. Most cybercrime is an attack on information about individuals, corporations or governments, although the attacks do not take place on a physical body, they do take place on the personal or corporate virtual body, which is the set of informational attributes that define people and institutions on the Internet.

In other words, in the digital age, our virtual identities are essential elements of everyday life. We are a bundle of numbers and identifiers in multiple computer databases owned by governments and corporations. Cybercrime highlights the centrality of networked computers in our lives, as well as the fragility of such seemingly solid facts as individual identity. So, this was the brief introduction of cybercrime. Now let's learn about the types of cybercrime that Black Hat Hackers performs.

Categories of Cybercrime

There are three major categories that cybercrime falls into: individual, property, and government. The types of methods used and difficulty levels vary depending on the category.

Property: This is similar to the case of criminals illegally obtaining an individual's bank or credit card information. Hackers steal someone's banking information to access money, make online purchases, or perform deceptive scams to trick people into giving away their information. They can also use malware to access websites containing confidential information.

Individual: This type of cybercrime involves someone spreading malicious or illegal information online. This may include cyberattacks, distribution of pornography and trafficking.

Government: This is the least common cybercrime, but also the most serious. Crimes against the government are also known as cyber terrorism. Government cybercrime includes hacking into government websites, military websites, or spreading propaganda. These criminals are usually terrorists or enemy governments of other countries.

Types of Cybercrime

Certainly, here are some common types of cybercrime listing below:

Cyberstalking refers to the use of digital communication tools, platforms, and online spaces to engage in persistent and unwanted harassment, monitoring, or threatening behavior towards an individual or group. This form of harassment can cause significant emotional distress, anxiety, and fear for the victim. Cyberstalking involves a range of activities that can be both invasive and harmful. Here are some key aspects of cyberstalking:

Methods and Activities:

Harassment: Cyberstalkers repeatedly send unwanted messages, emails, or comments to the victim, often with derogatory language, threats, or offensive content.

Monitoring: Stalkers may closely monitor the victim's online activities, including social media posts, comments, photos, and interactions, without the victim's consent.

Impersonation: Cyberstalkers might create fake profiles or accounts to impersonate the victim or spread false information about them.

Threats: Threatening messages, emails, or posts are commonly used by cyberstalkers to intimidate and frighten the victim.

Doxing: This involves revealing private or sensitive information about the victim, such as their address, phone number, or personal details, with the intent to harm or embarrass them.

Online Defamation: Cyberstalkers may spread false and damaging information about the victim, tarnishing their reputation and causing emotional distress.

Platforms and Channels:

Cyberstalking can occur across various digital platforms and communication channels, including:

- Social media platforms (Facebook, Twitter, Instagram, etc.)
- Email and messaging apps
- Online forums and communities
- Blogs and personal websites
- Online gaming platforms

Impact on Victims:

The effects of cyberstalking can be severe, leading to emotional and psychological distress. Victims may experience:

- Anxiety, fear, and paranoia
- Sleep disturbances and reduced quality of life
- Loss of privacy and personal security
- Social isolation and withdrawal from online activities
- Impaired mental well-being and self-esteem

Legal Implications:

Cyberstalking is considered a criminal offense in many jurisdictions, and laws are in place to protect individuals from this form of harassment. Depending on the severity and frequency of the stalking behavior, legal consequences can include restraining orders, fines, and even imprisonment.

Prevention and Response:

Protect Personal Information: Be cautious about sharing personal information online and adjust privacy settings on social media platforms.

Block and Report: Use platform features to block and report cyberstalkers. Document evidence of harassment.

Inform Authorities: If the stalking behavior escalates or becomes threatening, report the incidents to law enforcement.

Seek Support: Reach out to friends, family, or mental health professionals for emotional support.

It's essential to take cyberstalking seriously and to address it promptly to protect the well-being and safety of victims in the digital age.

Software Piracy:

Now, let's learn one of the most crime, cybercrime, which is software piracy, software piracy is the illegal copying, distribution or use of software. It is such a profitable business that it has caught the attention of organized crime groups in a number of countries. According to the Business Software

Alliance BSA, about 36 percent of all software in current use is stolen.

Let's see what is software piracy, software piracy has become a worldwide issue with China, the United States and India being the top three offenders, the commercial value of pirated software is 19 billion dollars in North America and Western Europe and has reached twenty-seven point three billion dollars in the rest of the world.

According to the 2018 Global Software Survey, 37 percent of software installed on personal computers is unlicensed software.

Software piracy doesn't require a hacker or a skilled coder, any normal person with a computer can become a software pirate if they don't know about the software laws with such a widespread impact.

It's important to understand what software piracy is and the dangers it presents. When you purchase a commercial software package, an end user license agreement, ULA is included to protect that software program from copyright infringement, typically the license states that you can install the original copy of software you bought on one computer and that you can make a backup copy in case the original is lost or damaged.

You agree to the licensing agreement when you open the software package? This is called a shrink wrap license. When you open the envelope that contains the software disks or when you install the software.

Software piracy applies mainly to full function commercial software, the time limited or function restricted versions of commercial software called shareware are less likely to be pirated since they are freely available.

Similarly, freeware, a type of software that is copyrighted but freely distributed at no charge, also offers little incentive for piracy.

Let's see types of software piracy, one soft lifting, the most common type of piracy, soft lifting, also called soft loading, means sharing a program with someone who is not authorized by the license agreement to use it.

A common form of soft lifting involves purchasing a single licensed copy of software and then loading the software onto several computers in violation of licensing terms on college campuses. It is rare to find a software program that has not been soft loaded.

People regularly lend programs to their roommates and friends, either not realizing it's wrong or not thinking that it's a big deal. Soft lifting is common in both businesses and homes.

Two hard disk loading often committed by hardware dealers; this form of piracy involves loading an unauthorized copy of software onto a computer being sold to the end user.

This makes the deal more attractive to the buyer at virtually no cost to the dealer. The dealer usually does not provide the buyer with manuals or the original CDs of the software. This is how operating systems like Windows 95 are often pirated.

Three, renting, renting involves someone renting out a copy of software for temporary use without the permission of the copyright holder.

The practice, similar to that of renting a video from Blockbuster, violates the license agreement of software. For OEM, unbundling often just called unbundling this form of piracy means selling standalone software originally meant to be included with a specific accompanying product.

An example of this form of piracy is someone providing drivers to a specific printer without authorization.

Five, counterfeiting, counterfeiting means producing fake copies of a software making it look authentic.

This involves providing the box CDs and manuals all designed to look as much like the original product as possible.

Microsoft products are the ones most commonly counterfeited because of their widespread use.

Most commonly, a copy of a CD is made with a CD burner, and a photocopy of the manual is made counterfeit software sold on street corners and sometimes unknowingly sold even in retail stores.

Counterfeit software sold at prices far below the actual retail price. Last but not the least, online piracy, the fastest growing form of piracy is Internet piracy, with a growing number of users online and with the rapidly increasing connection speeds, the exchange of software on the Internet has attracted an extensive following in the past bulletin board systems.

Beeb's were the only place where one could download pirated software. Currently, there are hundreds of thousands of Web sites providing unlimited downloads to any user. Often the software provided through these Web sites is cracked to eliminate any copy protection schemes.

Let's see what are the dangers of online piracy, software piracy may have a cheaper price point, but there are many dangers that software pirates should be aware of.

Consequences of software piracy are increased chances that the software will malfunction or fail, forfeited access to support for the programs such as training upgrades, customer support and bug fixes. No warranty and the software can't be updated, increased risk of infecting your PC with malware, viruses or adware slowed down PC. Legal repercussions due to copyright infringement using pirated software carries high penalties under copyright law for users caught in the act in the United States, copyright infringement can lead to up to five years in jail and a dollar of 250000 fine. The owner of the software is copyright can also sue for damages, which can run as high as 150000 dollars per copy tech while a dotcom. Tip of the video is keeping your PC secure by only purchasing software from authorised dealers, be aware of any software's terms and conditions. Make sure you agree and adhere to their guidelines.

Phishing:

It's time to learn one of the most performed cyber-attack that is phishing. Phishing is a cybercrime in which a target or targets are contacted by email, telephone or text message

by someone posing as a legitimate institution to lure individuals into providing sensitive data such as personally identifiable information, banking and credit card details and passwords.

The information is then used to access important accounts and can result in identity theft and financial loss.

The first phishing lawsuit was filed in 2004 against a California teenager who created the imitation of the website America Online with this fake Web site.

He was able to gain sensitive information from users and access the credit card details to withdraw money from their accounts other than email and Web site phishing.

There's also phishing, voice phishing, smooshing, SMS phishing and several other phishing techniques cyber criminals are constantly coming up with. Phishing is a cyber-attack that uses disguised email as a weapon.

The goal is to trick the email recipient into believing that the message is something they want or need

a request from their bank, for instance, or a note from someone in their company and to click a link or download an attachment.

What really distinguishes fishing is the form the message takes the attackers masquerade as a trusted entity of some kind, often a real or plausibly real person or a company the victim might do business with.

It's one of the oldest types of cyber-attacks dating back to the 1990s, and it's still one of the most widespread and pernicious, with phishing messages and techniques becoming increasingly sophisticated.

Common features of phishing emails, one too good to be true lucrative offers an eye catching or attention-grabbing statements are designed to attract people's attention immediately.

For instance, many claims that you have won an iPhone, a lottery or some other lavish prize. Just don't click on any suspicious emails.

Remember that if it seems too good to be true, it probably is true sense of urgency.

A favorite tactic among cyber criminals is to ask you to act fast because the super deals are only for a limited time.

Some of them will even tell you that you have only a few minutes to respond. When you come across these kinds of emails, it's best to just ignore them. Sometimes they will tell you that your account will be suspended unless you update your personal details immediately. Most reliable organizations give ample time before they terminate an account, and they never ask patrons to update personal details over the Internet. When in doubt, visit the source directly rather than clicking a link in an email.

Three hyperlinks.

A link may not be all it appears to be hovering over a link shows you the actual URL where you will be directed upon clicking on it. It could be completely different, or it could be a popular Web site with a misspelling for attachments. If you see an attachment in an email you weren't expecting or that doesn't make sense, don't open it. They often contain payloads like ransomware or other viruses. The only file type that is always safe to click on is a text file.

Five unusual senders. Whether it looks like it's from someone you don't know or someone you do know, if anything seems out of the ordinary, unexpected, out of character or just suspicious in general, don't click on it.

Let's see how you can protect yourself from being attacked, one, to protect against spam mails, spam filters can be used generally. The filters assess the origin of the message.

The software used to send the message and the appearance of the message to determine if it's spam.

Occasionally, spam filters may even block emails from legitimate sources. So, it isn't always 100 percent accurate.

To the browser settings should be changed to prevent fraudulent websites from opening browsers, keep a list of fake websites and when you try to access the Web site, the address is blocked or an alert message has shown the settings of the browser should only allow reliable websites to open up.

Three many Web sites require users to enter login information while the user image is displayed, this type of system may be open to security attacks.

One way to ensure security is to change passwords on a regular basis and never use the same password for multiple accounts. It's also a good idea for Web sites to use a CAPTCHA system for added security. For banks and financial organizations use monitoring systems to prevent phishing, individuals can report phishing to industry groups where legal actions can be taken against these fraudulent websites.

Organizations should provide security awareness training to employees to recognize the risks.

Five changes in browsing habits are required to prevent phishing. If verification is required, always contact the company personally before entering any details online.

Six If there is a link in an email hover over the Eurail first secure websites with a valid secure socket layer SSL certificate begin with https. Eventually all sites will be required to have a valid SSL. So, this is how you can protect yourself from being hacked.

Computer Hacking

It's time to learn computer hacking, cybercrime, so let's start computer hacking. It is a practice of modifying computer hardware and software to accomplish a goal outside the creator?

The purpose of hacking a computer system may vary from simply demonstrations of the technical ability to ceiling modifying or destroying information for social, economic or political reasons.

Now, the corporate are hiring hackers, a person who is engaged in hacking computers to intentionally hack the computer of an organization to find and fix security vulnerabilities.

The hackers may be classified as one white hat white hat hackers are the persons who hacked the system to find the security vulnerabilities of a system and notified to the organizations so that a preventive action can be taken to protect the system from outside hackers.

White hat hackers may be paid employee of an organization who is employed to find the security loopholes or may be a freelancer who just wants to prove his mantle in this field. They are popular, known as ethical hackers.

Two black hats, in contrast to the white hat, the black hat hacked the system with ill intentions.

They may hack the system for social, political or economically motivated intentions.

They find the security loopholes, the system, and keep the information themselves and exploit the system for personal or organizational benefits to an organization whose system is compromised, is aware of this and apply security patches. They are popularly known as crackers.

Three gray hat, grey hat hackers find out the security vulnerabilities and report to the site administrators and offer the fix of the security bug for a consultancy fee. So, this was all about computer hacking.

Computer Virus:

Spreading a virus is cybercrime. Let's get into it.

A computer virus is a computer program that can infect other computer programs by modifying them in such a way as to include a possibly evolved copy of it.

Note that a program does not have to perform outright damage, such as deleting or corrupting files in order to be called a virus.

Many people use the term loosely to cover any sort of program that tries to hide its malicious function and tries to spread onto as many computers as possible, viruses are very dangerous. They are spreading faster than they are being stopped. And even the least harmful of viruses could be fatal.

For example, a virus that stops a computer and displays a message in the context of a hospital life support computer could be fatal. Even the creator of a virus cannot stop it once it is in the wild.

The main types of PC viruses, generally, there are two main classes of viruses, the first class consists of the file and factors which attach themselves to ordinary program files.

These usually infect arbitrary Commodore ETEC programs, though some can infect any program for which execution is requested, such as Sess Auvil, PRG and Menu Files. File effectors can be either direct action or resident.

A direct action virus selects one or more other programs to infect each time the program that contains it is executed, a resident virus hides itself somewhere in memory, the first time an infected program is executed and thereafter infects other programs when they are executed, as in the case of the Jerusalem 185 virus or when certain other conditions are fulfilled. The Vienna virus is an example of a direct-action virus. Most other viruses are resident.

The second category is system or boot record effectors, those viruses that infect executable code found in certain system areas on a disk which are not ordinary files on DAST systems, there are ordinary boot sector viruses which infect only the downspout sector and MVR viruses which infect the master boot record on fixed disks and the dust boot sector on diskettes.

Examples include brain stoned empire, Azusa and Michelangelo. Such viruses are always resident viruses. Finally, a few viruses are able to infect both.

The Tukwila virus is one example.

These are often called multiple day viruses, though there has been criticism of this name.

Another name is blood and file virus.

File system or cluster viruses, for example, dear to me are those that modify directory table entries so that the virus is loaded and executed before the desired program is.

Note that the program itself is not physically altered, only the directory entry is.

Some consider these inspectors to be a third category of viruses, while others consider them to be a subcategory of the file inspectors.

Stealth virus, a stealth virus, is one that hides the modifications it has made in the file or Boot record, usually by monitoring the system functions used by programs to read files or physical blocks from storage media and forging the results of such system functions so that programs which try to read these areas see the original uninfected form of the file instead of the actual infected form. Thus, the viral modifications go undetected by antiviral programs.

However, in order to do this, the virus must be resident in memory when the antiviral program is executed.

The very first virus brain, a boot sector infector, monitors physical disk I o and redirects any attempt to read a brain infected boot sector to the disk area where the original boot sector is stored. The next viruses to use this technique with a file effectors number of the beast and Frodo.

Polymorphic virus, a polymorphic virus, is one that produces varied copies of itself in the hope that virus scanners will not be able to detect all instances of the virus, the most sophisticated form of polymorphism discovered so far as the mutation engine written by the Bulgarian virus writer who calls himself the Dark Avenger.

Fast and slow in factors, a typical file infector such as the Jerusalem copies itself to memory when a program infected by it is executed and then infects other programs when they are executed.

A fast infector is a virus which, when it is active in memory, infects not only programs which are executed, but also those which are merely opened.

The result is that if such a virus is in memory, running a scanner or integrity checker can result in all, or at least many programs becoming infected all at once.

The term slow infector is sometimes used for a virus that, if it is active in memory, infects only files as they are modified or created.

The purpose is to fool people who use integrity checkers into thinking that the modification reported by the integrity checker is due solely to legitimate reasons. An example is the Darth Vader virus.

Ultimately, spreading viruses and malware is the crime and it can harm your life. So, this is all about spreading computer virus.

Spamming

What is spamming email is both an excellent communication tool and also a way that companies can inform you about their latest products and services.

However, email is frequently used to deliver unwanted material, which is at best annoying and at worst malicious, causing considerable harm to your computer and yourself. Spam or junk email?

Always be vigilant when receiving or responding to emails, make sure your spam filter is always switched on to minimize the risks.

The vast majority of emails sent every day is unsolicited junk mail. Examples include advertising, for example, online pharmacies, pornography, dating, gambling, get rich quick and work from home schemes, hoax virus warnings, hoax charity appeals chain emails which encourage you to forward them to multiple contacts, often to bring good luck.

How spammers obtain your email address, one using automated software to generate addresses to enticing people to enter their details on fraudulent websites, three hacking into legitimate websites to gather users' details for buying email lists from other spammers.

Five, inviting people to click through to fraudulent websites posing as spam email cancellation services from names, addresses in the SEC line or in the body of emails which have been forwarded and the previous participants have not been deleted.

Avoid forwarding on joke emails.

You'll lose the very act of replying to a spam email confirms to spammers that your email address exists.

How to spot spam emails may feature some of the following warning signs like you don't know the sender, one contains misspellings, for example, P zero R and with a zero designed to fool spam filters to makes an offer that seems too good to be true. If it seems too good to be true, it probably is.

Three The subject line and contents do not match for contains an urgent offer.

End date for example, by now and get 50 percent off five contains a request to forward an email to multiple people and may offer money for doing so. Six contains a virus warning.

Seven contains attachments which could include XY files. The risks. It can contain viruses and spyware. It can be a tool for online fraud, such as phishing. Unwanted email can contain offensive images.

Manual filtering and deleting is very time consuming. It takes up space in your inbox. Email scams, scams are generally delivered in the form of a spam email, but remember, not all spam emails contain scams. Scams are designed to trick you into disclosing information that will lead to defrauding you or stealing your identity. **Be smart**. **Stay safe**.

Examples of email scams include emails offering financial, physical or emotional benefits, which are in reality linked to a wide variety of frauds.

These include emails posing as being from trusted sources such as your bank, the Inland Revenue, or anywhere else that you have an online account.

They ask you to click on a link and then disclose personal information, even take controls of your computer or network.

Online Scams

Online scams are deceptive schemes carried out over the internet with the aim of defrauding individuals, stealing sensitive information, or extracting money from victims. These scams exploit the anonymity and connectivity of the online world to trick users into believing false narratives, promises, or opportunities. Online scams can take various forms, targeting unsuspecting individuals through emails, social media, websites, and other digital channels.

Common Types of Online Scams:

Phishing Scams: Scammers send fraudulent emails, messages, or websites that mimic legitimate organizations to trick recipients into revealing personal information, such as passwords, credit card details, or login credentials.

Advance Fee Fraud: Victims are promised a substantial reward, inheritance, or business opportunity in exchange for a fee upfront. The promised reward never materializes, and the scammer disappears after collecting the payment.

Online Shopping Scams: Fake online stores offer attractive deals on products, collect payments, but never deliver the purchased items. Victims lose both their money and personal information.

Romance Scams: Scammers develop online romantic relationships, gain victims' trust, and then request money for various reasons like emergencies or travel expenses.

Tech Support Scams: Scammers pose as tech support personnel, claiming to help with computer issues. They trick victims into granting remote access to their devices and charge fees for fake services.

Lottery and Prize Scams: Victims receive notifications claiming they've won a lottery or prize. To claim the winnings, they are asked to pay fees or share personal information.

Investment Scams: Scammers promise high returns on investments, cryptocurrencies, or trading platforms, convincing victims to invest money. The investments are often fake or lead to losses.

Job and Employment Scams: Fake job offers require victims to pay upfront fees for background checks, training, or equipment. Legitimate jobs are rarely provided.

Charity Scams: Scammers pose as charitable organizations, seeking donations for fake causes or disasters, diverting funds from legitimate charities.

Online scams can cause financial losses, emotional distress, and compromise personal security. Staying vigilant, informed, and cautious when interacting online is crucial to protecting oneself from falling prey to these deceptive schemes.

These are just a few examples of the many types of cybercrime that exist. As technology advances, new forms of cybercrime continue to emerge, highlighting the importance of robust cybersecurity measures and vigilance in the digital realm.

Impact of Cybercrime on Society

Cybercrime has a profound impact on society, affecting individuals, businesses, governments, and the overall digital ecosystem. Its consequences can be wide-ranging and have both immediate and long-term effects. Here's an overview of the impact of cybercrime on society:

Financial Losses:

Cybercrime results in significant financial losses for individuals, businesses, and governments. Stolen funds, fraudulent transactions, and the costs of mitigating cyberattacks can drain resources and disrupt economic stability.

Data Breaches and Privacy Violations:

Data breaches compromise sensitive personal and financial information. Stolen data can be used for identity theft, fraud, and other criminal activities, leading to violations of privacy and loss of personal trust.

Disruption of Critical Services:

Cyberattacks on critical infrastructure, such as power grids, water supply systems, and transportation networks, can lead to widespread service disruptions and even endanger public safety.

Intellectual Property Theft:

Businesses and research institutions face the theft of intellectual property, trade secrets, and proprietary information. This theft can result in financial losses, loss of competitive advantage, and inhibited innovation.

Ransomware Extortion:

Ransomware attacks can paralyze businesses and organizations, causing operational disruptions and financial losses. Victims may be forced to pay ransoms to regain access to their data.

Economic Impact:

Cybercrime undermines economic growth by diverting resources from productive activities to cybersecurity efforts, incident response, and recovery. It can lead to decreased consumer trust in online transactions and digital services.

Reputational Damage:

Organizations that fall victim to cybercrime can suffer reputational damage, eroding trust among customers, partners, and stakeholders. Public perception of a brand's security measures can significantly influence consumer decisions.

Psychological Impact:

Individuals can experience anxiety, stress, and emotional distress as a result of cyberbullying, online harassment, or the loss of personal data. Cybercrime-induced psychological trauma can have lasting effects on mental health.

National Security Threats:

Cyberattacks targeting government institutions and agencies can compromise national security. Espionage, information warfare, and cyber-attacks on critical infrastructure can have far-reaching geopolitical implications.

Loss of Productivity:

Businesses and individuals may experience downtime, loss of productivity, and disrupted operations due to cyber incidents. This can lead to financial losses and hinder overall economic productivity.

Costs of Cybersecurity Measures:

The need to invest in cybersecurity measures to prevent and respond to cybercrime imposes additional financial burdens on businesses and governments. These costs can impact budget allocations for other essential services.

Erosion of Digital Trust:

Widespread cybercrime erodes public trust in digital technologies, online services, and electronic transactions. This mistrust can hinder the growth and adoption of digital innovations.

In summary, cybercrime's impact on society is far-reaching, affecting individuals' privacy, businesses' operations, and the overall stability of digital ecosystems. The increasing sophistication of cyber threats calls for concerted efforts from individuals, organizations, governments, and international bodies to strengthen cybersecurity measures, enhance legal frameworks, and raise awareness to mitigate the adverse effects of   cybercrime.

CHAPTER 5

AUTHENTICATION IN CYBERSECURITY: ENSURING DIGITAL IDENTITY AND SECURITY

In the ever-expanding digital landscape, where information flows seamlessly across networks and devices, the need for robust security measures has never been more critical. At the forefront of these measures stands authentication – a cornerstone of cybersecurity that safeguards digital interactions, protects sensitive data, and ensures the integrity of online transactions. This section delves into the concept of authentication, its significance, various methods, and its role in mitigating cyber threats.

Understanding Authentication:

Authentication is the process of verifying the identity of an entity, such as a user, device, or application, before granting access to a system, network, or resource. It is a fundamental security mechanism that prevents unauthorized individuals or entities from gaining entry to sensitive information or services. Authentication serves as the digital equivalent of presenting identification to access a physical facility.

The Level of Authentications

In the realm of cybersecurity, where the protection of digital assets and sensitive information is paramount, the concept of authentication has evolved to meet the growing sophistication of cyber threats. One notable advancement is the implementation of three-level authentication, a robust security measure that goes beyond traditional methods to provide an extra layer of protection. In this section, we delve into the intricacies of three-level authentication, its components, advantages, and its role in safeguarding digital identities.

Understanding Three-Level Authentication:

Three-level authentication, often referred to as "3FA" or "triple-factor authentication," takes the concept of multi-factor authentication (MFA) a step further by adding an additional layer of verification. MFA itself is a security protocol that requires users to provide two or more factors of authentication before accessing a system or resource. Three-level authentication builds upon this by incorporating a third factor, thereby enhancing security.

Components of Three-Level Authentication:

Something You Know: This is the traditional factor in authentication and typically involves a password, PIN, or passphrase that the user knows. It serves as the initial layer of security.

Something You Have: The second factor involves possessing a physical item or token that can generate temporary codes. This could be a smartphone, a hardware token, or a smart card.

Something You Are: The third and most advanced factor involves biometric data unique to the individual, such as fingerprints, facial scans, or iris patterns. Biometric authentication adds a high level of certainty to identity verification.

Advantages of Three-Level Authentication:

Enhanced Security: By adding an extra layer of verification, three-level authentication significantly reduces the risk of unauthorized access, data breaches, and cyber-attacks.

Protection Against Stolen Credentials: Even if a malicious actor gains access to one or two factors, the presence of the third factor makes unauthorized access substantially more difficult.

Mitigation of Impersonation: Biometric data, as the third factor, is incredibly challenging to replicate, reducing the chances of impersonation or fraud.

Three-Level Authentication in Practice:

Imagine a scenario where a user is attempting to access a highly sensitive government database. In addition to entering their password (something they know) and providing a one-time code generated by their smartphone (something they have), they are also required to undergo a facial recognition scan (something they are). Only when all three factors are successfully verified will the user gain access to the database.

This triple-layered approach ensures that even if an attacker manages to obtain the password and the smartphone, they cannot bypass the biometric verification.

Embracing Enhanced Security:

To implement three-level authentication effectively, organizations must prioritize user experience alongside security. This involves integrating user-friendly biometric recognition technologies, facilitating seamless generation of temporary codes, and ensuring ease of use for all levels of users.

In an era where cyber threats continue to evolve, three-level authentication stands as a formidable defense against unauthorized access and data breaches. By incorporating the dimensions of something you know, something you have, and something you are, this advanced security measure bolsters the protection of digital identities and sensitive information, fortifying the digital landscape against the ever-present threat of cyber-attacks.

The Importance of Authentication: Safeguarding Digital Interactions and Data

In an age characterized by the seamless flow of information and the rapid advancement of technology, the importance of authentication in cybersecurity cannot be overstated. Authentication serves as the guardian of our digital world, ensuring that only authorized individuals gain access to sensitive information, systems, and services. This section delves into the significance of authentication, its key role in protecting digital interactions, and its role in mitigating the risks posed by cyber threats.

1. Verifying Identity and Preventing Unauthorized Access:

At its core, authentication is about verifying the identity of individuals, devices, or applications seeking access to a system or resource. By confirming that the requester is indeed who they claim to be, authentication prevents unauthorized access by malicious actors seeking to exploit vulnerabilities. This is particularly crucial in environments where data confidentiality and integrity are paramount, such as financial institutions, healthcare systems, and government databases.

2. Protecting Sensitive Data:

Authentication serves as the first line of defense against data breaches. When properly implemented, it prevents unauthorized users from gaining access to sensitive information, safeguarding personal, financial, and proprietary data from falling into the wrong hands. This protection is of utmost importance in an era marked by the increasing frequency and sophistication of cyber-attacks targeting valuable data assets.

3. Mitigating Cyber Threats:

Cyber threats, ranging from phishing attacks to ransomware, consistently pose significant risks to individuals and organizations alike. Proper authentication mechanisms significantly reduce the attack surface by ensuring that malicious actors cannot easily infiltrate systems and networks. By requiring multiple factors of authentication, such as passwords, biometric data, or tokens, the potential for unauthorized access or exploitation of vulnerabilities is dramatically curtailed.

4. Strengthening Regulatory Compliance:

Various industries are subject to strict regulatory frameworks that mandate the protection of sensitive information. Authentication not only aligns with these regulations but also demonstrates a commitment to data security. Compliance with regulations such as the General Data Protection Regulation (GDPR) and the Health Insurance Portability and Accountability Act (HIPAA) often requires robust authentication measures to ensure the confidentiality and privacy of personal data.

5. Building User Trust:

Authentication is also vital for building and maintaining user trust. In an era where online transactions, communication, and interactions are commonplace, individuals expect their digital interactions to be secure and private. Strong authentication practices reassure users that their sensitive information is being handled responsibly, fostering a sense of confidence in the organizations they engage with.

6. Balancing Convenience and Security:

While the primary focus of authentication is security, it also plays a role in user experience. Striking the right balance between stringent security measures and user convenience is essential. The implementation of user-friendly authentication methods, such as biometric recognition or single sign-on (SSO) solutions, ensures that security measures do not impede productivity or frustrate users.

Authentication is the cornerstone of cybersecurity, ensuring that digital interactions remain secure and private in an interconnected world. By verifying identities, preventing unauthorized access, protecting sensitive data, and mitigating cyber threats, authentication empowers individuals and organizations to navigate the digital landscape with confidence. As the digital realm continues to evolve, the importance of authentication remains steadfast, anchoring the foundation of a secure and trustworthy online ecosystem.

Methods of Authentication

Password-Based Authentication: The most common method involves users providing a unique combination of characters (password) that only they should know. However, passwords can be vulnerable to breaches if weak or compromised.

Multi-Factor Authentication (MFA): This approach requires users to provide two or more pieces of evidence to verify their identity. Common factors include something the user knows (password), something they have (smartphone or token), and something they are (biometric data like fingerprints).

Biometric Authentication: Utilizes unique physical traits, such as fingerprints, facial features, or iris scans, to confirm identity. Biometrics offer high security but require specialized hardware.

Token-Based Authentication: Involves using physical or software-based tokens that generate temporary codes. These codes change regularly and must be used within a specific timeframe.

Certificate-Based Authentication: Uses digital certificates to authenticate users, devices, or applications. Certificates are issued by a trusted authority and are difficult to forge.

Behavioral Authentication: Analyzes user behavior patterns, such as typing speed and mouse movements, to determine if the behavior aligns with the legitimate user's profile.

Authentication in Action: A Glimpse into Secure Digital Interactions

Imagine logging into your online banking account. You enter your username (something you know) and your password (another thing you know). However, to enhance security, the bank also requires a fingerprint scan (something you are) from your smartphone (something you have). This process is an example of multi-factor authentication, as it combines three different factors to verify your identity before granting access to sensitive financial information.

Scenario 1: Online Banking

Imagine you're logging into your online banking account to review your transactions and manage your finances. As you enter your username and password, you're engaging in password-based authentication. This initial layer verifies that you are the legitimate account holder. However, to enhance security, your bank employs multi-factor authentication (MFA). After entering your password, you receive a one-time code on your smartphone (something you have). This code, often sent via text message or through a mobile app, serves as the second authentication factor. The combination of something you know (password) and something you have (smartphone) ensures a robust verification process before granting access to your financial information.

Scenario 2: Airport Security Screening

At the airport, you approach a self-service kiosk to check in for your flight. The kiosk employs biometric authentication to enhance security and streamline the check-in process. You place your finger on a fingerprint scanner, and the system compares your fingerprint data to a stored template. If the fingerprints match, you're granted access to your boarding pass and flight information. Biometric authentication, in this case, serves as both an identity verification method and a convenience factor, reducing the need for physical documents and speeding up the check-in process.

Scenario 3: Secure Corporate Network Access

You're a remote employee trying to access your company's internal network to collaborate on a project. The company employs token-based authentication for secure network access. You use a hardware token provided by the company, which generates a time-sensitive code. After entering your username and password, you input the code from the hardware token. The token generates a new code at regular intervals, and the system verifies its accuracy. This multi-factor authentication process, involving something you know (password) and something you have (hardware token), ensures that only authorized personnel can access the company's sensitive data and resources.

Scenario 4: Mobile App with Single Sign-On (SSO)

You're using a mobile app that offers various services, from email to social media. The app employs single sign-on (SSO) functionality. When you log in with your credentials, the app securely authenticates your identity. Once authenticated, you can seamlessly access different services within the app without needing to enter your credentials repeatedly. SSO enhances user convenience while maintaining security by minimizing the exposure of login information.

CHAPTER 6

ENCRYPTION IN CYBERSECURITY: SECURING THE DIGITAL WORLD WITH UNBREAKABLE SHIELDS

In the realm of cybersecurity, where the protection of sensitive data and communications is paramount, encryption stands as a formidable shield against the prying eyes of cybercriminals and unauthorized entities. Encryption transforms information into an unreadable format, ensuring that only authorized parties with the corresponding decryption keys can access and decipher the content. This section delves into the intricacies of encryption, its significance, methods, and its pivotal role in fortifying digital security.

Understanding Encryption?

At its core, encryption is the process of converting plaintext (original data) into ciphertext (encrypted data) using mathematical algorithms and encryption keys. The ciphertext appears as a jumbled sequence of characters, making it virtually impossible for unauthorized entities to comprehend without the decryption key. Encryption is the cornerstone of data protection, guarding against eavesdropping, data breaches, and unauthorized access.

The Importance of Encryption

Confidentiality: Encryption ensures that sensitive information remains confidential, even if intercepted by malicious actors during transmission or storage.

Data Integrity: Encryption safeguards data from tampering or alteration during transit, as any unauthorized modification would render the decryption process impossible.

Authentication: Encryption can also be used to verify the authenticity of a sender. A digital signature, generated using the sender's private key, confirms that the message or data originated from the expected source.

Methods of Encryption

Symmetric Encryption: In this method, a single secret key is used for both encryption and decryption. While efficient, securely sharing the key with authorized parties poses a challenge.

Asymmetric Encryption (Public Key Encryption): This method employs a pair of keys – a public key for encryption and a private key for decryption. Data encrypted with the public key can only be decrypted using the corresponding private key, enhancing security and eliminating the need to share a secret key.

Hashing: While not strictly encryption, hashing is a one-way cryptographic function that generates a fixed-length output (hash) based on input data. Hashes are used for data integrity verification but cannot be reversed to reveal the original data.

Consider sending an email containing sensitive financial information to your accountant. Before transmission, you encrypt the email using your accountant's public key. Only your accountant, possessing the private key, can decrypt and read the contents. During transit, even if intercepted, the ciphertext remains unintelligible without the private key.

Best Practices for Encryption: Safeguarding Digital Assets with Expert Precision

In the intricate tapestry of cybersecurity, encryption stands as a vital thread, woven to protect sensitive data from the ever-present threats of cybercriminals and unauthorized access. However, the effectiveness of encryption lies not only in its implementation but also in the adherence to best practices that ensure its strength and resilience. Here, we delve into the essential best practices for encryption, guiding organizations and individuals toward a fortified digital defense.

1. Choose Strong Encryption Algorithms: Selecting robust encryption algorithms forms the bedrock of effective data protection. Opt for established and widely recognized algorithms such as the Advanced Encryption Standard (AES) for symmetric encryption and RSA for asymmetric encryption. These algorithms have undergone extensive scrutiny and validation by the cryptographic community.

2. Regularly Update Encryption Keys: Encryption keys are the keys to the digital vault. Regularly update and rotate encryption keys to mitigate the risk posed by compromised keys. When a key becomes outdated or compromised, all data encrypted with that key remains secure.

3. Protect Encryption Keys: Safeguard encryption keys with the utmost care. Use secure key management practices, such as hardware security modules (HSMs) or software-based solutions, to prevent unauthorized access or theft of keys.

4. Implement End-to-End Encryption: For communication applications, deploy end-to-end encryption. This ensures that messages are encrypted on the sender's side and decrypted only on the recipient's side. Even service providers cannot access the decrypted content.

5. Encrypt Data at Rest: Protect data stored on devices, servers, and databases by encrypting it. This prevents unauthorized access to sensitive information, even if the physical storage medium is compromised.

6. Secure Communication Channels: When transmitting data over networks, use secure communication protocols like HTTPS for web traffic or VPNs for remote access. Secure communication channels enhance the protection of data in transit.

7. Educate Users: Raise awareness among users about the importance of encryption and its proper usage. Train them to recognize secure communication channels and verify websites using SSL certificates.

8. Regularly Update Software: Ensure that the software and tools you use for encryption are up to date. Updates often include security patches that address vulnerabilities and enhance encryption strength.

9. Conduct Periodic Security Audits: Regularly assess the effectiveness of your encryption practices through security audits. Identify any weaknesses or vulnerabilities and take proactive measures to address them.

10. Maintain Compliance: Adhere to relevant industry regulations and compliance standards that require encryption of specific types of data. Compliance not only ensures data protection but also avoids legal and financial repercussions.

11. Monitor for Anomalies: Implement monitoring and alert systems that can detect unusual or suspicious activities related to encrypted data. This proactive approach allows for swift response to potential threats.

12. Regular Backups: While not a direct encryption practice, maintaining regular backups of encrypted data is crucial. In the event of data loss or corruption, backups ensure that valuable information can be recovered.

Encryption is a potent weapon in the arsenal of cybersecurity. By following these best practices, organizations and individuals can fortify their digital defense and ensure that sensitive data remains beyond the reach of malicious actors. The commitment to implementing and maintaining encryption best practices underscores the responsibility we all share in safeguarding our digital world from the ever-present threats of the cyber realm.

How Does Encryption Work?

The process of encryption involves a delicate interplay of mathematical operations and cryptographic keys:

Plaintext and Encryption Key: The process begins with the plaintext data that needs to be protected. Simultaneously, an encryption key is generated or chosen. The encryption key is a unique string of characters that determines how the plaintext will be transformed into ciphertext.

Mathematical Transformation: The encryption algorithm, often a complex mathematical function, takes the plaintext and the encryption key as input. The algorithm performs a series of mathematical operations, rearranging the data according to the key's instructions.

Ciphertext Generation: The output of the encryption algorithm is the ciphertext. This ciphertext is a seemingly random sequence of characters that appears as gibberish to anyone who lacks the corresponding decryption key. The ciphertext bears no resemblance to the original plaintext, making it exceedingly difficult for unauthorized individuals to reverse-engineer the original data.

Decryption Key and Decryption Algorithm: To reverse the encryption process and retrieve the original plaintext, a decryption key is required. This key is a complementary counterpart to the encryption key. The decryption algorithm, which mirrors the encryption algorithm, uses the decryption key to reverse the mathematical operations performed during encryption.

Decryption: When the correct decryption key is applied to the ciphertext using the decryption algorithm, the original plaintext is reconstituted. The decryption process effectively unlocks the sealed box, revealing the contents to authorized individuals.

Encryption in Everyday Scenarios

Secure Online Transactions: When you enter your credit card information on an e-commerce website, encryption ensures that your financial details are transmitted in an encrypted format, protecting them from interception by cybercriminals.

Email Privacy: Email services often employ encryption to safeguard the contents of your emails. Only the intended recipient possessing the appropriate decryption key can read the message.

Data Storage: Encrypting files or folders on your computer or mobile device ensures that even if your device is lost or stolen, the data remains inaccessible without the decryption key.

Encryption's magic lies in its mathematical complexity and the secure interplay between encryption and decryption keys. Through this process, sensitive data is rendered impervious to unauthorized access, ensuring that only those with the correct keys can unlock and comprehend the contents. In a digital landscape fraught with cyber threats, encryption emerges as the unsung hero, safeguarding our private communications, financial transactions, and sensitive information, fortifying the digital realm against the ever-present specter of data breaches and unauthorized access.

Exploring the Best Encryption Algorithms: Building a Fortified Digital Defense

In the intricate landscape of cybersecurity, encryption algorithms serve as the bedrock of data protection, ensuring that sensitive information remains impervious to prying eyes and cyber threats. The effectiveness of encryption lies in the choice of algorithms, and here we delve into some of the best encryption algorithms that stand as pillars of security in the digital realm.

Advanced Encryption Standard (AES):

Widely regarded as one of the most secure encryption algorithms, AES has become the gold standard for symmetric encryption. AES operates by dividing data into blocks and applying a series of complex mathematical operations. It offers three key lengths—128, 192, and 256 bits—and is used extensively to secure communications, data at rest, and more.

RSA (Rivest-Shamir-Adleman):

Asymmetric encryption relies on RSA, an algorithm that uses a pair of keys—a public key for encryption and a private key for decryption. RSA is particularly effective for secure key exchange and digital signatures. Its security is based on the difficulty of factoring large semiprime numbers, ensuring its robustness against brute-force attacks.

Elliptic Curve Cryptography (ECC):

ECC is a modern asymmetric encryption technique that offers strong security with shorter key lengths compared to RSA. This makes ECC particularly suited for resource-constrained environments like mobile devices and IoT devices. ECC leverages elliptic curves to provide strong encryption and efficient computation.

Triple Data Encryption Standard (3DES):

3DES is an enhancement of the original Data Encryption Standard (DES) algorithm, which became vulnerable to brute-force attacks due to its small key size. 3DES applies the DES algorithm three times in succession with different keys, significantly enhancing security. However, due to its computational intensity, 3DES is being phased out in favor of more efficient algorithms.

Blowfish:

Designed by Bruce Schneier, Blowfish is a symmetric block cipher that offers a fast and secure encryption method. It supports key lengths ranging from 32 to 448 bits, making it adaptable to various security requirements. While not as widely used as AES, Blowfish remains a strong option for certain applications.

Twofish:

Developed as a successor to Blowfish, Twofish is another symmetric block cipher known for its security and efficiency. Twofish operates on 128-bit blocks and supports key lengths up to 256 bits. While not as widely adopted as AES, Twofish's robustness and flexibility make it a noteworthy choice.

ChaCha20:

ChaCha20 is a stream cipher designed to provide high-speed encryption with strong security. It is often used in applications where efficient encryption is crucial, such as securing internet communication. ChaCha20's simplicity, speed, and resistance to certain types of attacks make it a popular choice.

Camellia:

Camellia is a symmetric block cipher developed jointly by Japan and Europe. It supports key lengths of 128, 192, and 256 bits, and its design incorporates elements from AES and SEED (a Korean encryption algorithm). Camellia offers a high level of security and has gained recognition in various international standards.

In the ever-evolving landscape of cybersecurity, the selection of encryption algorithms plays a pivotal role in safeguarding digital assets and information. These best encryption algorithms represent the culmination of decades of cryptographic research and development, offering strong security measures to defend against the multitude of threats present in the digital realm. By employing these trusted algorithms, organizations and individuals can build a fortified digital defense that stands resilient against the challenges of the cyber landscape.

Best Practices for Encryption

Certainly, I'd be happy to provide you with some best practices for encryption. Encryption is a crucial aspect of maintaining data security and privacy, whether it's in transit or at rest. Here are some key practices to follow:

Use Strong Encryption Algorithms: Choose encryption algorithms that are widely recognized and considered secure, such as AES (Advanced Encryption Standard) for symmetric encryption and RSA or ECC (Elliptic Curve Cryptography) for asymmetric encryption.

Key Management: Ensure proper key management practices. Store encryption keys separately from the data they protect. Use key vaults or hardware security modules (HSMs) for added protection.

Key Length and Complexity: Use encryption keys with appropriate lengths. Longer keys generally provide higher security. For example, AES-256 uses a 256-bit key length.

Regularly Update Keys: Rotate encryption keys at regular intervals. If a key is compromised, the damage will be limited if the key changes frequently.

Use Perfect Forward Secrecy (PFS): In protocols like TLS (Transport Layer Security), enable PFS to ensure that compromising a single session's private key doesn't lead to the compromise of previous or subsequent sessions.

SSL/TLS Certificates: Use valid SSL/TLS certificates for encrypting data in transit. Keep certificates up to date and avoid using self-signed certificates in production environments.

Data at Rest Encryption: Encrypt data stored in databases, file systems, or cloud storage. Most modern database systems offer options for transparent data encryption.

Secure Key Exchange: When using asymmetric encryption, use secure methods for exchanging public keys, such as using well-established key distribution mechanisms or key servers.

Implement Two-Factor Authentication (2FA): Use 2FA to add an additional layer of security, even if encryption is compromised.

Use Authenticated Encryption: Choose encryption modes that provide both confidentiality and authenticity, such as GCM (Galois/Counter Mode) or CCM (Counter with CBC-MAC).

Secure Algorithms for Passwords: When dealing with password-based encryption, use secure password hashing algorithms like bcrypt or Argon2.

Keep Software Updated: Keep encryption libraries and software up to date to ensure any vulnerabilities are patched.

Audit and Monitoring: Implement logging and monitoring to detect any unauthorized access or suspicious activities related to encryption keys or data.

Secure Initialization Vectors (IVs): If your encryption mode requires an initialization vector, make sure it's generated securely and is unique for each encryption operation.

Secure Random Number Generation: Use cryptographically secure random number generators for generating keys, IVs, and other cryptographic elements.

Avoid Homegrown Encryption: Avoid creating your own encryption algorithms or protocols. Stick to established standards that have undergone thorough review.

Threat Modeling: Regularly assess your system's threat landscape to identify potential weaknesses in your encryption strategy.

Secure Coding Practices: Implement secure coding practices to prevent vulnerabilities that could lead to encryption bypass or data leaks.

Disposal of Keys and Data: When keys or encrypted data are no longer needed, ensure they are properly disposed of using secure deletion methods.

Training and Awareness: Educate your team about encryption best practices and the importance of maintaining security throughout the data lifecycle.

Remember that encryption is just one part of an overall security strategy. It's important to adopt a layered approach to security that includes practices such as access control, intrusion detection, and regular security assessments.

CHAPTER 7

DIGITAL SIGNATURES IN CYBERSECURITY: FORTIFYING IDENTITY AND TRUST

In the vast realm of cybersecurity, where secure digital transactions and communication are paramount, digital signatures stand as a beacon of trust and authenticity. These cryptographic signatures, much like their physical counterparts, serve to validate the identity of a sender and ensure the integrity of digital documents and messages. This article delves into the intricacies of digital signatures, shedding light on their significance, mechanisms, and role in bolstering cybersecurity.

What Are Digital Signatures?

At its core, a digital signature is a cryptographic mechanism that combines the concepts of identity authentication, data integrity, and non-repudiation. It involves the use of encryption techniques to create a unique digital imprint that is affixed to electronic documents, messages, or transactions.

This imprint serves as a digital seal, indicating both the origin of the content and its unaltered state.

Understanding Digital Signatures

A digital signature is a cryptographic technique that combines the concepts of authentication and data integrity. It involves a process where a sender's identity is verified, and a unique digital imprint is applied to the document or message. This imprint, akin to a seal, ensures that the content remains unaltered during transmission and attests to the identity of the sender.

How Digital Signatures Work

The process of creating and verifying digital signatures involves several key steps:

Hashing: The content of the document or message is first hashed—a process that generates a fixed-size string of characters unique to that specific content. Even a minor alteration in the content will result in a vastly different hash value.

Private Key: The sender uses their private key to encrypt the hash value. The private key is known only to the sender and ensures that the signature is unique to them.

Digital Signature: The encrypted hash, along with other information, constitutes the digital signature. This signature is attached to the document or message, serving as proof of the sender's identity and the integrity of the content.

Public Key Verification: To verify the digital signature, the recipient uses the sender's public key to decrypt the encrypted hash value. If the decrypted hash matches the newly computed hash of the received content, the signature is valid, and the content remains unaltered.

The Significance of Digital Signatures

Authentication: Digital signatures authenticate the identity of the sender. A valid digital signature confirms that the content was indeed sent by the claimed sender.

Data Integrity: By using cryptographic hashes, digital signatures ensure that the content has not been altered during transmission. Any modification to the content would result in a mismatch between the decrypted hash and the recalculated hash.

Non-Repudiation: Digital signatures provide non-repudiation, meaning the sender cannot later deny sending the content. This is because the private key is unique to the sender.

Real-World Applications

Secure Documents: Digital signatures are used to sign electronic documents, contracts, and agreements, ensuring their authenticity and integrity.

Emails: Email encryption and digital signatures authenticate the sender and protect the content from tampering.

Contract Signing: In the business world, digital signatures facilitate the signing of contracts and agreements in a secure and legally recognized manner.

E-commerce Transactions: Digital signatures provide assurance during online transactions, assuring the authenticity of payment requests and receipts.

Software Distribution: Digital signatures are applied to software packages to verify their origin and integrity, protecting users from downloading malicious software.

In an age where digital interactions are integral to business, communication, and everyday life, digital signatures serve as a linchpin of cybersecurity. By providing identity verification, data integrity, and non-repudiation, digital signatures instill trust in digital transactions and communications, fortifying the digital landscape against the persistent threat of cybercrime and unauthorized access.

CHAPTER 8

ANTIVIRUS IN CYBERSECURITY: THE SHIELD AGAINST MALICIOUS INTRUSIONS

In the realm of cybersecurity, where the battle between defenders and attackers rages incessantly, antivirus software emerges as a stalwart sentinel, guarding digital domains against the relentless onslaught of malware and cyber threats. This article delves into the world of antivirus, unraveling its significance, mechanisms, and role in fortifying digital defenses.

Antivirus software, often simply referred to as **"antivirus,"** is a cybersecurity solution designed to detect, prevent, and eliminate malicious software, commonly known as malware. Malware encompasses a wide spectrum of digital threats, including viruses, worms, Trojans, ransomware, and spyware. The primary function of antivirus software is to identify and neutralize these threats to protect computers, networks, and data.

How does it work?

Antivirus software employs several mechanisms to detect and combat malware:

Signature-Based Detection: This method involves maintaining a database of known malware signatures. When the antivirus scans a file or system, it compares the signatures to those in its database. If a match is found, the software identifies the file as malicious.

Heuristic Analysis: Antivirus software uses heuristic algorithms to identify potentially suspicious behavior or characteristics exhibited by files or programs. This enables the software to detect previously unknown malware that may not have established signatures.

Behavioral Analysis: Some advanced antivirus solutions analyze the behavior of files and programs. If a program exhibits behavior commonly associated with malware, such as unauthorized data access or replication, the antivirus may flag it for further investigation.

Sandboxing: Antivirus software may use isolated environments called sandboxes to execute suspicious files or programs. If the file behaves maliciously within the sandbox, it is considered a potential threat and is dealt with accordingly.

The Importance of Antivirus

Malware Prevention: Antivirus software acts as a bulwark against the proliferation of malware, stopping malicious software from infiltrating systems and networks.

Timely Detection: Antivirus solutions swiftly identify and neutralize threats, minimizing the potential damage caused by malware.

Data Protection: By preventing malware infections, antivirus software safeguards sensitive data from theft, corruption, or unauthorized access.

Mitigation of Malicious Activity: Antivirus software aids in blocking malicious activities, such as unauthorized data transmission or unauthorized access to system resources.

Applications in Real-World:

Shielding Digital Realms from Malicious Threats

In the dynamic landscape of modern technology, where digital interactions are integral to daily life, the real-world applications of antivirus software extend far and wide, safeguarding individuals, businesses, and organizations from the pervasive threat of malicious software. This article delves into the practical applications of antivirus software, shedding light on how it fortifies digital realms and protects against an array of cyber threats.

Personal Devices: Antivirus software is a fundamental addition to personal computers, laptops, and mobile devices. Its applications include:

- Malware Prevention: Antivirus software ensures that users' devices are shielded from malware, such as viruses, worms, and Trojans, when browsing the internet, downloading files, or using applications.

- Safe Online Transactions: Antivirus software safeguards financial and personal information during online banking and shopping, preventing phishing attacks and identity theft.

- Malicious Attachment Detection: It scans email attachments and downloaded files to prevent unwitting exposure to malware through emails or downloaded content.

Enterprise Security: In the business world, antivirus software plays a pivotal role in maintaining a secure digital environment:

- **Network Protection:** Antivirus solutions are deployed across networks to safeguard data, servers, and communication channels against malware attacks that could disrupt operations or compromise sensitive information.

- **Data Breach Prevention:** By identifying and neutralizing malware, antivirus software helps prevent data breaches and leaks, safeguarding proprietary information and customer data.

- **Remote Work Security:** With the rise of remote work, antivirus software ensures that devices used for remote access adhere to security standards, preventing potential breaches through unsecured connections.

Email Security: Antivirus software contributes to secure communication by enhancing email security:

- **Attachment Scanning:** It scans email attachments for malware, ensuring that users do not inadvertently open malicious files that could compromise their devices.

- **Link Protection:** Antivirus software can flag suspicious links in emails, protecting users from phishing attempts and fraudulent websites that aim to steal sensitive information.

Website Security: Antivirus software extends its reach to web browsing:

- Safe Browsing: Some antivirus programs offer browser extensions that warn users about potentially harmful websites, preventing them from visiting malicious or phishing sites.

Ransomware Defense: As ransomware attacks escalate, antivirus software plays a critical role in mitigation:

- Ransomware Detection: Antivirus solutions monitor for ransomware behaviors, preventing the execution of malicious code that could encrypt valuable data and demand a ransom for its release.

IoT Protection: In the era of the Internet of Things (IoT), antivirus software extends its defense to interconnected devices:

- **Securing Smart Devices:** Antivirus solutions safeguard smart devices, such as smart home appliances, wearables, and IoT devices, preventing cybercriminals from exploiting vulnerabilities in these devices.

Software Verification: Antivirus software ensures the authenticity of downloaded software:

- **Software Verification:** It scans downloaded software packages for potentially harmful code or unauthorized modifications, protecting users from installing malicious or counterfeit applications.

From personal devices to sprawling corporate networks, antivirus software stands as a digital guardian, tirelessly defending against the myriad threats that lurk in the digital realm. By preventing malware infections, ensuring safe online transactions, and fortifying communication channels, antivirus software empowers individuals and organizations to navigate the digital landscape with confidence. As cyber threats continue to evolve, the real-world applications of antivirus software remain essential in upholding the principles of cybersecurity and preserving the integrity and privacy of digital interactions.

FARHADUR RAHIM

CHAPTER 9

THE GUARDIAN AT THE GATEWAY: UNDERSTANDING FIREWALLS

In the ever-expanding digital landscape, where information flows freely across networks, the role of firewalls emerges as a pivotal element in safeguarding digital domains from the relentless onslaught of cyber threats. Firewalls stand as the guardian at the gateway, tasked with filtering, monitoring, and managing the flow of data between trusted and untrusted networks. In this chapter, we will delve deep into the realm of firewalls, exploring their significance, mechanisms, types, and real-world applications.

One of the major challenges that companies face when trying to secure their sensitive data is finding the right tools for the job, even for a common tool such as a firewall, sometimes called a network firewall.

Many businesses might not have a clear idea of how to find the right firewall or firewalls for their needs, how to configure those firewalls, or why such firewalls might be necessary.

Yes, now, what is a firewall, a firewall is a type of cybersecurity tool that is used to filter traffic on a network, firewalls can be used to separate network nodes from external traffic sources, internal traffic sources or even specific applications.

Firewalls can be software, hardware or cloud based, with each type of firewall having its own unique pros and cons.

The primary goal of a firewall is to block malicious traffic requests and data packets while allowing legitimate traffic through.

Firewall Different Types and Mechanisms: How They Work

Firewall types can be divided into several different categories based on their general structure and method of operation, here are eight types of firewalls, one packet filtering firewalls, two circuit level gateways, three stateful inspection firewalls for application level gateways, a.k.a. proxy firewalls, next gen firewalls. software firewalls. hardware firewalls, cloud firewalls.

A firewall can be implemented using hardware as well as software or the combination of both.

Hardware Firewalls: example of hardware firewalls are routers through which the network is connected to the network outside the organization i.e. Internet.

Software Firewalls: These firewalls are installed and installed on the server and client machines and it acts as a gateway to the organizations" network.

In the operating system like Windows 2003, Windows 2008 etc. it comes embedded with the operating system. The only thing a user need to do is to optimally configure the firewall according to their own requirement. The firewalls can be configured to follow "**rules**" and "**policies**" and based on these defined rules the firewalls can follow the following filtering mechanisms. Let's know how do these firewalls work and which ones are the best for your business?

Packet filtering firewall as the most basic and oldest type of firewall, architecture, packet filtering firewalls basically create a checkpoint in a traffic router or switch.

The firewall performs a simple check of the data packets coming through the router inspecting information. Such as the destination and origination IP address, packet type, port number and another surface level information without opening up the packet to inspect its contents. If the information packet doesn't pass the inspection, it is dropped.

The good thing about these firewalls is that they aren't very resource intensive. This means they don't have a huge impact on system performance and are relatively simple. However, there are also relatively easy to bypass compared to firewalls with more robust inspection capabilities.

Circuit level gateways as another simplistic firewall type that is meant to quickly and easily approve or deny traffic without consuming significant computing resources. Circuit level gateways work by verifying the transmission control protocol TCP handshake.

This TCP handshake check is designed to make sure that the session the packet is from is legitimate. While extremely resource efficient, these firewalls do not check the packet itself. So, if a packet held malware, they had the right TCP handshake, it would pass right through. This is why circuit level gateways are not enough to protect your business by themselves.

Stateful inspection firewalls, these firewalls combined both packet inspection technology and TCP handshake verification to create a level of protection greater than either of the previous two architectures could provide a alone. However, these firewalls do put more of a strain on computing resources as well. This may slow down the transfer of legitimate packets compared to the other solutions.

Proxy firewalls application level gateways, cloud firewalls, proxy firewalls operated the application

layer to filter incoming traffic between your network and the traffic source, hence the name application level gateway.

These firewalls are delivered via a cloud-based solution or another proxy device. Rather than letting traffic connect directly, the proxy firewall first establishes a connection to the source of the traffic and inspects the incoming data packet. This check is similar to the stateful inspection firewalls in that it looks at both the packet and at the TCP handshake protocol.

However, proxy firewalls may also perform deep layer packet inspections, checking the actual contents of the information packet to verify that it contains no malware. Once the check is complete and the packet is approved to connect to the destination, the proxy sends it off. This creates an extra layer of separation between the client, the system where the packet originated and the individual devices on your network.

Let's steering them to create additional anonymity and protection for your network. If there's one drawback to proxy firewalls, it's that they can create significant slowdown because of the extra steps in the data packet transferal process.

Next generation firewalls many of the most recently released firewall products are being touted as next generation architectures.

However, there is not as much consensus on what makes a firewall truly next, General. Some common features of Next-Generation Firewall architectures include deep packet inspection, checking the actual contents of the data packet.

TCP handshake checks and surface level packet inspection Next-Generation Firewalls may include other technologies as well, such as intrusion prevention systems, eyepieces that work to automatically stop attacks against your network. The issue is that there is no one definition of a next generation firewall, so it's important to verify what specific capabilities such firewalls have before investing in one.

Cloud firewalls whenever a cloud solution is used to deliver a firewall, it can be called a cloud firewall or firewall as a service FOSE. Cloud firewalls are considered synonymous with proxy firewalls by many, since a cloud server is often used in a proxy firewall set up, though, the proxy doesn't necessarily have to be on the cloud. It frequently is.

The big benefit of having cloud-based firewalls is that they are very easy to scale with your organization. As your needs grow, you can add additional capacity to the cloud server to filter larger traffic loads, cloud firewalls like hardware firewalls, excellent perimeter security.

Web Application Firewalls (WAF) Focused on web application security, WAFs protect web servers and applications from a range of attacks, such as cross-site scripting and SQL injection.

Application Layer Filtering, advanced firewalls scrutinize the content of data packets at the application layer, identifying and blocking malicious or unauthorized content.

The Importance of Firewalls: Safeguarding Digital Frontiers

At its core, a firewall is a barrier designed to protect a network or device from unauthorized access while permitting legitimate communication to flow unhindered. Much like the physical walls of a fortress, firewalls form a line of defense, inspecting incoming and outgoing traffic to ensure that only authorized entities are granted entry.

The importance of firewalls emerges as the basis of protecting sensitive information and critical systems. Firewalls, like watchful guards, stand guard at the digital frontier, organizing defenses against the relentless wave of cyber threats. This section explores the profound importance of firewalls in consolidating digital domains and maintaining the integrity of data and communications.

Network Security Bastion:

At its core, the firewall serves as a digital bastion, erected to shield networks from unauthorized access and potential breaches. By controlling the flow of data traffic between trusted internal networks and external, potentially hostile domains, firewalls act as the gatekeepers, meticulously filtering incoming and outgoing information. This defensive stance ensures that only legitimate and authorized connections are established, preventing malicious actors from infiltrating networks.

Intrusion Detection and Prevention:

Firewalls not only control data flow but also act as vigilant monitors. Through intrusion detection and prevention systems, advanced firewalls scrutinize network traffic for anomalies, patterns indicative of cyber-attacks, and unauthorized access attempts. By promptly identifying such threats, firewalls play a pivotal role in thwarting attacks before they breach the network's defenses, enhancing overall security posture.

Protection from Malware:

In an environment where malware proliferates with alarming frequency, firewalls offer a potent defense against its ingress. By inspecting data packets for signs of malicious code, firewalls can prevent malware-laden files from entering the network. This proactive stance curtails the spread of viruses, worms, and Trojans that can compromise systems, corrupt data, and disrupt operations.

Application Layer Security:

Firewalls extend their protection beyond mere packet filtering by engaging in application layer security. This approach involves scrutinizing the content of data packets at a deeper level, ensuring that applications adhere to security protocols and are devoid of exploitable vulnerabilities. By doing so, firewalls thwart attacks like cross-site scripting (XSS) and SQL injection that target application vulnerabilities.

Regulatory Compliance:

In a landscape rife with data protection regulations and compliance requirements, firewalls play a pivotal role in helping organizations adhere to these mandates. By safeguarding sensitive data from unauthorized access and potential breaches, firewalls contribute to the confidentiality and privacy standards mandated by regulations like GDPR, HIPAA, and PCI DSS.

Mitigation of Denial-of-Service (DoS) Attacks:

Firewalls provide a defense against disruptive denial-of-service attacks that inundate networks with an overwhelming volume of traffic, rendering them inaccessible. Through intelligent traffic analysis, firewalls can identify and mitigate these attacks, ensuring that critical services remain available to users.

Secure Remote Access:

In the era of remote work and mobile connectivity, firewalls ensure secure remote access to internal resources. Virtual Private Network (VPN) firewalls authenticate remote users and encrypt their connections, safeguarding data transmission from potential eavesdropping or interception.

Business Continuity:

By protecting networks from cyber threats and potential breaches, firewalls contribute to the continuity of business operations. Uninterrupted operations bolster stakeholder trust, prevent financial losses, and maintain the integrity of services.

In a digital landscape characterized by both boundless opportunities and persistent threats, firewalls assume a role of paramount importance. They stand as the first line of defense, fortifying digital realms against unauthorized access, malicious intrusions, and cyber-attacks. By combining vigilant monitoring, intelligent filtering, and proactive prevention, firewalls preserve the integrity of data, communication, and digital infrastructure.

Applications in Real-World

In a world where the preservation of digital trust is paramount, the significance of firewalls in upholding the pillars of cybersecurity cannot be overstated.

Firewalls find their place in diverse scenarios across industries:

Enterprise Networks: Firewalls are deployed in corporate networks to safeguard sensitive data, prevent data breaches, and regulate employee internet usage.

Home Networks: Consumers use firewalls to protect their personal devices and data from online threats, ensuring a safe online experience.

Cloud Security: Firewalls play a crucial role in cloud environments, securing data and applications hosted on remote servers.

Industrial Control Systems (ICS): In critical infrastructure sectors like energy and manufacturing, firewalls protect industrial control systems from cyber-attacks that could disrupt essential operations.

Challenges and Considerations

While firewalls provide robust security, challenges include:

Advanced Threats: Some sophisticated attacks can bypass traditional firewalls, necessitating the integration of advanced threat detection and response mechanisms.

Traffic Encryption: Encrypted traffic can be challenging to inspect, as it conceals the content from traditional firewall analysis.

CHAPTER 10

INTRODUCTION TO STEGANOGRAPHY

Steganography is a sophisticated and ancient technique of data concealment that goes beyond mere encryption, aiming to achieve covert communication by hiding sensitive information within seemingly innocuous carriers, such as images, audio files, text, or other digital data formats. Derived from the Greek words "steganos" (meaning "covered" or "hidden") and "graphein" (meaning "to write"), steganography encompasses a wide array of methods and strategies that enable the embedding of confidential content within a host medium, thereby obscuring the existence of the hidden data from unintended recipients.

The primary objective of steganography is to ensure clandestine communication while evading detection. Unlike encryption, which transforms the content into an unreadable form, steganography seeks to maintain the cover medium's appearance as unchanged as possible, making it challenging for adversaries to identify the presence of concealed information. This distinct feature sets steganography apart from encryption, which typically relies on making data unreadable through mathematical transformations or algorithms.

Throughout history, various techniques have been employed for steganographic purposes. These techniques can be broadly categorized into spatial domain methods, which involve altering the pixel values of an image, and frequency domain methods, which manipulate the image's Fourier or wavelet transform coefficients. Additionally, text-based steganography can involve modifying the arrangement of letters or words within a text document, audio steganography can involve manipulating sound frequencies, and video steganography can involve subtly altering the frames of a video sequence.

The utilization of steganography is not solely confined to the digital realm; it has historical roots that extend to physical forms of communication as well. Ancient civilizations employed techniques such as invisible ink, microdots, and hidden messages within artwork to convey covert information. In the modern era, the proliferation of digital data and the advent of high-capacity storage and transmission technologies have exponentially expanded the potential applications of steganography.

While steganography can be utilized for legitimate purposes such as safeguarding sensitive data, it also presents challenges for law enforcement and cybersecurity professionals. Malicious actors can exploit steganographic techniques to hide malware, exfiltrate data, or coordinate cyberattacks. Consequently, detection mechanisms and forensic tools have been developed to identify potential instances of steganography and thwart illicit activities.

The Significances of Steganography

The importance of steganography stems from its capacity to address vital requirements in the realms of security, privacy, and covert communication. This technique holds significance in a variety of contexts and applications:

Confidentiality: Steganography plays a crucial role in maintaining the confidentiality of sensitive information. By hiding data within innocuous carriers, individuals and organizations can exchange crucial data without drawing attention to its existence, reducing the risk of interception by unauthorized parties.

Security: Steganography provides an additional layer of security beyond encryption. While encryption protects data by rendering it unreadable, steganography obscures the very presence of the data. This added layer of concealment can make it exceedingly challenging for malicious actors to even identify that hidden information is being communicated.

Covert Communication: In scenarios where overt communication is risky or prohibited, steganography offers a clandestine means of exchanging information. Activists, whistleblowers, and individuals under surveillance can utilize steganography to bypass potential monitoring and ensure that their messages reach the intended recipients discreetly.

Counterterrorism and Law Enforcement: Law enforcement agencies can leverage steganalysis techniques to uncover hidden messages and detect potential threats, aiding in counterterrorism efforts. Detecting steganography enables authorities to identify and prevent criminal activities that may otherwise go unnoticed.

Digital Watermarking: Steganography is employed in digital watermarking, a technique used to embed imperceptible information into media files (such as images, audio, or video) to verify authenticity, trace copyright ownership, and prevent unauthorized distribution.

Data Exfiltration: For cybercriminals, steganography can be misused to conceal the theft of sensitive data, as it allows them to surreptitiously transfer information out of secure environments without arousing suspicion.

Privacy Preservation: In the era of pervasive surveillance and data collection, steganography can safeguard individual privacy. By concealing personal data within digital content, users can control what information is shared and limit the potential for intrusive data analysis.

Information Warfare: In military and intelligence contexts, steganography aids in information warfare by enabling covert communication, strategic deception, and manipulation of adversarie's perception of data.

Research and Development: Researchers employ steganography to develop and test methods for data concealment, thereby enhancing the field's understanding of vulnerabilities and defense mechanisms in digital communication.

Digital Forensics: Steganalysis, the practice of detecting and analyzing hidden information, is a critical aspect of digital forensics. It helps investigators uncover potential evidence hidden within media files during criminal investigations.

Educational and Ethical Use: In educational settings, steganography serves as a fascinating tool to explore the intricacies of data manipulation, cryptography, and digital security. Ethical hackers and security professionals also utilize steganography to assess vulnerabilities and strengthen information systems.

In essence, steganography provides a valuable arsenal of techniques that cater to the growing need for secure, covert communication in an interconnected world. Its applications span across security, law enforcement, privacy, research, and creative expression, highlighting its enduring significance in both the digital and real-world domains.

CHAPTER 11

INVESTIGATING CYBER CRIMES: INTRODUCTION TO COMPUTER FORENSIC

In an era characterized by relentless digitization and interconnectedness, the realm of law enforcement, cybersecurity, and investigations has undergone a profound transformation. At the heart of this transformation lies the fascinating and dynamic field of computer forensics. With a mandate to uncover hidden truths in the digital landscape, computer forensics serves as a crucial tool in solving cybercrimes, mitigating security breaches, and upholding justice in an evolving technological landscape.

Computer forensics, also known as digital forensics, is a multidisciplinary field within cybersecurity and law enforcement that involves the systematic examination, analysis, and preservation of digital evidence in order to investigate and reconstruct digital crimes, security breaches, and illicit activities. Rooted at the intersection of technology, law, and investigative methodologies, computer forensics serves as a critical tool for identifying, documenting, and attributing digital misdeeds, thereby aiding legal proceedings, incident response, and the pursuit of justice in the digital age.

The history of computer forensics traces the evolution of this specialized discipline from its early roots to its current role as a pivotal component of digital investigations, cybersecurity, and law enforcement efforts. The journey of computer forensics showcases the rapid advancement of technology and the corresponding need to adapt investigative techniques to the digital age.

1970s-1980s: Emergence of Digital Evidence

The origins of computer forensics can be traced back to the 1970s, when computers were becoming more accessible. Initially, law enforcement agencies recognized the potential of computers as sources of evidence in criminal investigations. Early efforts focused on the recovery of data from magnetic tapes and punched cards.

Late 1980s-1990s: Digital Crime and Response:

With the widespread adoption of personal computers and the growth of the internet, computer-related crimes began to emerge. The 1980s saw the rise of hacking incidents and computer viruses, prompting law enforcement to develop methods for investigating these new types of offenses.

The term **"computer forensics"** started to gain traction in the late 1980s and early 1990s. As digital evidence became more complex, professionals recognized the need for structured methodologies to recover, analyze, and present this evidence in court.

Mid-1990s: Legal Precedents:

In 1994, the case of United States v. Halper involved the admissibility of digital evidence in court. This case set an important legal precedent, establishing that electronic evidence could be used in court if certain criteria were met. This marked a crucial step in recognizing the validity and importance of digital evidence.

Late 1990s-2000s: Maturing Discipline:

As cybercrimes continued to evolve, so did the field of computer forensics. Tools and methodologies were refined to cope with the increasing complexity of digital evidence. The first computer forensics certifications were introduced, formalizing the training and expertise required for practitioners in the field.

The advent of high-capacity storage media, sophisticated file systems, and encryption posed new challenges for investigators. Digital evidence was no longer limited to traditional computers; mobile phones, storage devices, and networked systems became integral to investigations.

2000s-Present: Rise of Cybersecurity and Beyond:

The 2000s witnessed a surge in cyberattacks, data breaches, and online criminal activities. Computer forensics gained prominence as a critical component of incident response and cybersecurity efforts. Professionals began focusing on not just post-incident analysis, but also on proactive measures to prevent and mitigate digital threats.

The diversification of technology brought about new challenges in the form of cloud computing, IoT devices, and cryptocurrency transactions. As technology advanced, so did the methods and tools of computer forensics. Automated forensic tools, digital imaging, and specialized software became essential for managing large volumes of data.

Future Directions: AI and Emerging Technologies:

Looking ahead, the field of computer forensics continues to evolve. As artificial intelligence, machine learning, and blockchain technologies advance, computer forensics professionals are exploring new ways to extract, analyze, and interpret digital evidence.

The integration of AI algorithms could expedite the analysis of vast amounts of data, aiding investigators in identifying patterns, irregularities, and connections that may not be immediately apparent. Blockchain analysis is also becoming vital in tracking cryptocurrency transactions and addressing emerging challenges in the digital financial landscape.

In an increasingly digitized world, computer forensics addresses a wide range of objectives, including:

Evidence Identification: The primary objective of computer forensics is to identify potential sources of digital evidence. This includes pinpointing electronic devices, storage media, and data repositories that may contain information relevant to an investigation. Whether it's a computer, mobile phone, server, or cloud storage, identifying the sources is the initial step in the process.

Evidence Preservation: Once potential sources of evidence are identified; the next objective is to preserve the integrity of the digital evidence. This involves creating a forensically sound copy of the original data, ensuring that no alterations or modifications occur during the copying process. This copy becomes the basis for all subsequent analysis and investigation.

Data Recovery: In situations where data has been intentionally deleted, corrupted, or hidden, computer forensics aims to recover as much relevant information as possible. This may involve using specialized tools and techniques to restore deleted files, reconstruct data fragments, and piece together a coherent representation of the digital landscape.

Data Analysis: Computer forensics involves a meticulous analysis of the copied digital evidence. This analysis seeks to uncover patterns, relationships, timelines, and connections between various pieces of data. By scrutinizing files, logs, metadata, and system artifacts, investigators aim to reconstruct the sequence of events leading to the incident under investigation.

Malware Analysis: If malware is suspected to have been involved in a digital crime or security breach, one of the objectives of computer forensics is to analyze the malicious software. This involves dissecting the code, studying its behavior, identifying its propagation methods, and assessing its impact on affected systems.

Timeline Reconstruction: Creating an accurate timeline of events is essential in understanding the progression of a digital incident. Computer forensics professionals piece together actions, access times, modifications, and communications to reconstruct a coherent chronological sequence of events leading up to, during, and after the incident.

Attribution and Identification: Another key objective is to identify the individuals or entities responsible for the digital incident. Through careful analysis of digital footprints, access logs, communication records, and system interactions, investigators aim to attribute actions to specific users, devices, or groups.

Digital Chain of Custody: Maintaining a proper chain of custody is crucial in legal proceedings. Computer forensics professionals ensure that the digital evidence is handled, stored, and transported in a manner that preserves its integrity and admissibility in court.

Documentation and Reporting: Clear and thorough documentation is vital in computer forensics. Investigators produce detailed reports outlining their findings, methodologies, analysis techniques, and conclusions. These reports serve as essential documents in legal proceedings and internal investigations.

Legal Compliance: Computer forensics ensures that all investigations and evidence collection are conducted in adherence to legal standards, regulations, and privacy requirements. Adhering to these standards is essential to ensure that the evidence collected remains admissible in court.

Supporting Legal Proceedings: Ultimately, the objective of computer forensics is to provide tangible support to legal proceedings. The evidence and analysis produced by computer forensics professionals can be presented in court to establish guilt or innocence, support litigation, and facilitate the pursuit of justice.

Preventing Recurrence: Beyond investigations, computer forensics aims to contribute to prevention. By analyzing incidents, identifying vulnerabilities, and understanding attack vectors, organizations can take proactive measures to fortify their security defenses and reduce the likelihood of future incidents.

In summary, the objectives of computer forensics encompass the systematic identification, preservation, analysis, and documentation of digital evidence to uncover the truth, establish accountability, and facilitate legal proceedings. Through these objectives, computer forensics plays a pivotal role in ensuring the integrity of digital interactions, upholding cybersecurity, and maintaining the rule of law in the digital realm.

Computer Forensic Applications and Impact

The applications of computer forensics are far-reaching and diverse, impacting various sectors of society:

Cybercrime Investigations: Computer forensics is at the forefront of combating cybercrimes, ranging from data breaches and financial fraud to hacking and identity theft. Its methods are essential in tracing the digital footprints of criminals.

Incident Response: When a security breach occurs, computer forensics plays a pivotal role in containing the incident, understanding its scope, and facilitating recovery. Swift response is essential to minimize damage and protect sensitive information.

Law Enforcement Support: Law enforcement agencies rely on computer forensics to gather evidence for prosecuting cybercriminals and ensuring that justice prevails even in the digital realm.

Corporate Security: Organizations utilize computer forensics to investigate internal breaches, intellectual property theft, and employee misconduct. It assists in maintaining trust, safeguarding proprietary information, and enforcing security policies.

Civil Litigation: In civil cases, computer forensics uncovers evidence related to intellectual property disputes, trade secrets, contract breaches, and more. This evidence holds significance in legal battles where digital interactions are key.

Ethical Hacking: Computer forensics experts, known as ethical hackers or penetration testers, assess systems for vulnerabilities and weaknesses. Their insights enable organizations to bolster their defenses against potential threats.

FARHADUR RAHIM

Challenges and Future Trends

While computer forensics offers invaluable insights, it also faces challenges:

Encryption and Anonymity: The widespread use of encryption and anonymization tools presents difficulties in tracing digital activities and attributing actions to specific individuals.

Evolving Technology: Rapid technological advancements require computer forensics professionals to stay updated with the latest tools, techniques, and attack vectors.

Big Data and Cloud: With the exponential growth of data and the migration to cloud environments, handling and analyzing vast amounts of information poses challenges.

The future of computer forensics holds exciting prospects:

IoT Forensics: As the Internet of Things (IoT) expands, investigating interconnected devices will become critical, necessitating new methods for data extraction and analysis.

Blockchain Analysis: With the rise of cryptocurrencies and blockchain technology, forensic experts will explore methods to trace transactions and uncover illicit activities.

AI and Automation: Artificial intelligence and machine learning will likely be integrated into computer forensics tools, enhancing efficiency in evidence analysis and pattern recognition.

In a digital landscape where evidence is increasingly intangible and crimes are becoming more sophisticated, computer forensics stands as a beacon of truth. Its practitioners harness the power of technology, leverage legal expertise, and master investigative techniques to unveil hidden narratives. As the world navigates the complexities of the digital age, the field of computer forensics remains an essential guardian of justice, ensuring that even in a realm of anonymity and encryption, the truth will not remain hidden.

CHAPTER 12

CERTIFICATIONS ON CYBER SECURITY

Cyber-attacks are the fastest growing crime in the U.S. and they continue to grow in size and sophistication, companies like Facebook, Panera Bread, Under Armour and Uber made headlines after having customer information stolen with each breach. Administrative fears and the demand for cybersecurity analysts is increasing.

These fears are not unfounded, Center found that 66 percent of customers in the U.S. would likely halt any interaction with a business that's officially been hacked.

As a company, you might find yourself scrambling to hire top cybersecurity talent or equip your team with cybersecurity certifications as an I.T. professional.

The demand for cybersecurity skills presents a huge opportunity to boost your resume, stand out among candidates and increase your earning potential. But with so many IT security certifications out there, where do you start as the leading IT training company?

We compiled the top cybersecurity certifications IT professionals need to earn in 2019.

One certified ethical hacker, C.H. to computer security, plus three certified information systems security professional SIST for certified information security manager Cesme, five Certified Information Systems Auditor Cissé, six NYST Cybersecurity Framework and CSF seven certified cloud security professional SEECP eight Computer Hacking Forensic Investigator Seifi nine. Cisco Certified Network Associate SCANA Security.

Certified Ethical Hacker

One certified ethical hacker, S.H., to stop a hacker, you must be able to think like one. It's an interesting balance between toeing the line of moral actions and processing the malicious thoughts the average cyber-criminal would have.

This kind of mentality isn't easy to come by, which is why the certified ethical hacker course was created.

Real viruses, information security laws and standards chase students go through real time scenarios where they are exposed to different ways. Hackers penetrate networks and steal information. Students learn how to scan, test and hack and protect their systems.

IT professionals who complete this course have many positions to choose from, the most notorious being, penetration testing, penetration testing jobs require you to hack into a network without actually stealing any data.

This job function demands a high level of trust, which is well rewarded, penetration tester salaries often top out at just over 130000 dollars annually, according to pay scale.

The certification benefits security officers, auditors, security professionals, site administrators and anyone concerned about network infrastructure security.

Comptia Security+

To come to security plus computer security plus is a base level certification for IT professionals new to cybersecurity, you only need two years of IT experience to complete it.

The Kalmykia security plus certification is regarded as a general cybersecurity certification because it doesn't focus on a single vendor product line.

Network attack strategies and defenses, elements of effective security policies, network and host-based security, best practices, business continuity and disaster recovery, encryption standards and products, computer security plus is great for anyone looking to gain basic it's security knowledge.

It helps build a solid foundation that you can enhance with other courses.

The certification is so well respected that the U.S. Department of Defense mandates it for all employees. Because security applies to all levels and job roles, this course will also benefit application developers, PC support analysts and senior managers in accounting, sales and marketing roles.

Certified Information Systems Security Professional (CISSP)

Three certified information systems security professional susp, another popular certification for general cybersecurity knowledge is the Certified Information Systems Security Professional Course.

Many IT companies consider system a base requirement for employees responsible for network security.

To take this exam, you need at least three to five years of field experience, the system is considered the crown jewel of cybersecurity certifications, and passing the exam can lead to some incredibly lucrative positions. Security architects, for example, can make more than 150000 dollars annually.

The certification is a must have for people looking to move into a chief information security officer CISO role, but it's also a salary booster for analysts' systems engineers, consultants and IT security managers.

Other Certifications on Cyber Security

Certified Information Security Manager (CISM):

Also offered by (ISC)², the CISM certification is tailored for information security managers. It validates skills in managing and governing enterprise information security programs and focuses on risk management, incident response, and governance.

Certified Information Systems Auditor (CISA):

The CISA certification, also from (ISC)², is designed for professionals involved in auditing, control, and assurance of information systems. It focuses on auditing processes, risk management, and IT governance.

Certified Cloud Security Professional (CCSP):

Jointly offered by (ISC)² and the Cloud Security Alliance (CSA), the CCSP certification is aimed at individuals working with cloud technologies. It covers cloud architecture, governance, risk management, and compliance.

Cisco Certified CyberOps Associate:

This Cisco certification focuses on cybersecurity operations, providing foundational knowledge in security monitoring, incident response, network intrusion analysis, and security policies.

GIAC Security Essentials (GSEC):

The GSEC certification, provided by the Global Information Assurance Certification (GIAC), is designed for professionals seeking to demonstrate their knowledge of information security concepts and practices.

Certified Cybersecurity Professional (CCP):

The CCP certification, offered by the Australian Cyber Security Centre (ACSC), is recognized internationally. It covers core cybersecurity skills and is suitable for various roles within the field.

Certified Information Privacy Professional (CIPP):

The CIPP certification, from the International Association of Privacy Professionals (IAPP), focuses on privacy laws, regulations, and practices. It's particularly relevant for professionals dealing with data privacy and protection.

Offensive Security Certified Professional (OSCP):

The OSCP certification, offered by Offensive Security, is a hands-on and challenging certification for penetration testers. It involves passing a 24-hour practical exam to demonstrate practical skills in exploiting vulnerabilities.

Certified Incident Handler (GCIH):

The GCIH certification, provided by GIAC, focuses on incident handling and response. It is tailored for professionals dealing with the identification, containment, and recovery from security incidents.

These are just a few examples of the wide array of certifications available in the field of cybersecurity. When choosing a certification, consider your career goals, expertise level, and areas of interest within the field. Each certification provides a unique pathway to advancing your cybersecurity knowledge and contributing to the ever-growing challenge of securing digital assets and information.

CONCLUSION

In the dynamic and interconnected aspects of today's digital world, cyber security has emerged as an essential pillar of safeguarding individuals, organizations, and societies from the evolving threats that technology brings. For beginners embarking on their journey into the realm of cyber security, this field presents both exciting opportunities and significant responsibilities.

As you delve into the world of cyber security, remember that it encompasses a diverse array of concepts, practices, and disciplines. From understanding the fundamental principles of confidentiality, integrity, and availability to exploring encryption, firewalls, and intrusion detection systems, your exploration will be multifaceted.

Equipped with knowledge about different types of threats, such as malware, phishing, and social engineering, you'll be better prepared to recognize and mitigate potential risks. As you navigate this path, you'll discover that a proactive approach to security, which includes regular updates, strong passwords, and user awareness, is key to maintaining a robust defense against cyber threats.

In the realm of cyber security, continuous learning is not just encouraged—it's essential. Rapid advancements in technology mean that the landscape is in a constant state of flux, requiring you to stay current with emerging trends, vulnerabilities, and defense mechanisms. Engaging with online courses, certifications, and community forums will provide you with valuable insights and networking opportunities.

Remember that cyber security extends beyond technology; it's about understanding human behavior, ethics, and the legal implications of digital actions. A commitment to ethical behavior and respect for privacy will guide your decisions as you navigate this ever-evolving domain.

Whether you're a curious individual, a student, or a professional looking to transition into the field, your journey into cyber security begins with a curiosity to learn, a dedication to protect, and a determination to make the digital world a safer place for everyone.

As you take your first steps, embrace the challenges, remain open to learning, and celebrate each achievement along the way. The field of cyber security welcomes diverse perspectives and talents, and your contribution—no matter how big or small—has the potential to make a significant impact in a world that increasingly depends on the secure and responsible use of technology.

Cyber Security Overview for Absolute Beginners

ABOUT THE AUTHOR

Farhadur Rahim is a software engineer and technology enthusiast with a strong background in computer science, product design and entrepreneurship. He is passionate about building solutions that solve people's problems and enjoys learning and sharing his thoughts on new technologies around him. He has created some notable open source libraries and is a known leader for his contributions toward Javascript, PHP and numerous automations. Farhadur Rahim's professional career includes working both in the corporate company and in startups to create mockups, prototypes, launch new products, analyse metrics, and continually innovate.